hola

simply
delicioso

simply
delicioso

a collection of everyday recipes with a latin twist

ingrid
hoffmann

with raquel pelzel

Clarkson Potter/Publishers
New York

Copyright © 2008 by Ingrid Hoffmann
Photographs copyright © 2008 by Andrew Meade

Published in the United States by Clarkson Potter/Publishers, an imprint of the Crown Publishing Group, a division of
Random House, Inc., New York.
www.crownpublishing.com
www.clarksonpotter.com

Clarkson N. Potter is a trademark and Potter and colophon are registered trademarks of Random House, Inc.

Library of Congress Cataloging-in-Publication Data
Hoffmann, Ingrid.
    Simply delicioso: a collection of everyday recipes with a Latin twist / Ingrid Hoffmann. — 1st ed.
    Includes index.
    1. Cookery, Latin American.   I. Title.
TX716.A1H62   2007
641.598—dc22   2006102260

978-0-307-34734-3

Printed in Japan

Design by Elizabeth Van Itallie

10 9 8 7 6 5 4 3 2 1

First Edition

To Mom, Dad, Johanna, Annelies, Jossy, Andrew, Franco,
Diego, Joshua, and Tía Marlene.
Without you, life would not taste the same.

In memory of my grandparents, Hani, Tita, Tata, and Titita,
and Tía Chela and Yeyo. So many of the recipes in this book
inspire memories of you.

contents

preface

I consider myself a professional eater, and there is nothing in this world that I crave more than food. I live to eat and to cook real, everyday food—the kind of food we crave, the kind of food that just tastes good. To me, "simple" means "simply *delicioso,*" and that is how I approach each and every recipe in this book. Nothing gives me more pleasure than cooking and sharing my food with friends and family, and I want to encourage you to do the same.

I try to balance my two lives, my crazy work life and my even crazier personal life. You know, seeing my family, chatting up friends, and, most important, playing, loving, and living! God knows how tough it can be—and the last thing I want to end up doing is slaving in the kitchen. I mean, if cooking isn't fun and if the end result isn't totally satisfying, then why bother? This is my philosophy, and if I can stand by it while still making gratifying, satisfying meals, then you can, too.

Most of the ingredients I use are familiar ones, though I have snuck in a few surprises here and there that I'm really excited for you to get to know. Trust me, there's a reason why I add them to certain recipes. If you let me take you on a trip of discovery, I promise to introduce you to some really "wow!" flavors. For those of you who might already be familiar with the ajíes, mojos, and adobos of Latin cooking, then you'll learn some new *chica* tips, tricks, and shortcuts (and yes, even a few new recipes, too). It comes down to this: No matter how experienced you are with Latin food, you are in for a fun ride.

I grew up in my mom's kitchen. She is a Cordon Bleu–trained chef, a restaurant owner, and a caterer, and her passion for food was absolutely contagious. My culinary influences and rebellious style were without a doubt shaped by her creativity as well as by the many different continents that I have been fortunate enough to call home. Once you get to know me, you'll see I am a bit of a "mutt," having lived between Latin and American cultures in the United States, the Caribbean, Colombia, and other countries. Miami is now my home and has been for seventeen years. The way I cook is like a love affair between these two cultures, often spiked with a dash of homey Latin America and a pinch of haute America. I am living *la vida* Spanglish in all senses, and I have embraced these sides of my personality. So when it comes to food, you'd better believe that for me, it's about the burgers and beans all the way.

I don't follow a manual for cooking—or for making love, for that matter—and believe me, cooking is a labor of love! There is even a saying that goes *El amor entra por la cocina,* meaning, "Love comes in through the kitchen." If you cook from the soul, you can't go wrong.

Using techniques and formulas seems too much like sitting through high school calculus and algebra. I was tortured enough back then—I don't need to put myself through it now! Cookbooks are a place to turn to for fun, adventure, and inspiration. Take what you like from my recipes and create your own cross-cultural anthem. Breaking the rules is fun. Try it, you'll see!

When I was young I used to pull a stool over to the stove so I could reach the stovetop and cook up some really crazy concoctions. Oddly enough, on the first set of my television show I had to stand on a platform because the prep counter was built too high. How funny it is that some things never change! Since I first developed an interest in cooking, my family encouraged me, telling me that they loved my creations. But I know that deep down, they worried that I would cook when no one else was home and burn the house down! Lucky for all of us, I never did light our home ablaze—though I'm sure I did plenty of secret cooking when no one else was looking.

I have always been a rebel in the kitchen. So what? Who's going to come and get me, the food police? Freedom in the kitchen has helped me to create many of the recipes in this book, like my Hello Kitty Dressing (page 69) made with condensed milk, vinegar, and strawberries. I know it sounds funky, but just try it (and don't worry, there's no recipe for Snoopy sauce!).

My two sisters, Johanna and Annelies, weren't very good eaters, and my mother did not want to have to go through all of the food drama again with me—number three, and the baby. So she turned to everyone's favorite authority on children (back then, at least), Dr. Spock, and followed his advice on how to get your baby to love food and be a good eater. Boy, did it work! Not only did I grow up loving food, I became completely obsessed with it.

I don't know whether Dr. Spock cursed me or blessed me with this lifelong love affair with food. What I do know is that this book has been an incredible outlet for me to share my passion for simply *delicioso* food. Writing it was like pouring my hunger onto a keyboard. These dishes are my treasures. They're what I eat when I'm in love and when I'm single, when I'm happy and when I'm sad, feeling tired or craving a taste of home. Who said you have to be hungry to eat, anyway?

Every recipe takes me down memory lane to certain times in my life. Just like a song—but instead of hearing the lyrics and reminiscing, I'm tasting a dish and remembering a story, a place, or a person. Whether the recipes come from my television show *Simply Delicioso;* my columns in *BuenHogar* or *Rumbo*; my former restaurant, Rocca; or my mom, what all of them have in common is a practical, real approach to food.

Sure, I like to be traditional, too . . . when it's convenient! I've included some of my favorite takes on the Latin American standards as well as some spiced-up twists on non-Latin classics. You can rest assured not only that these recipes are *muy ricas*—very tasty—but that they work, too. I make these same meals for dinner with my family and friends—and I don't cook just anything for those cherished times. Everything in this book is cooked with love and passion from my heart and kitchen to yours. Being around a table, breaking bread, sharing food and laughter—to me, this is what life is all about. *La familia* that eats together stays together. And so this story of food, flavor, and life begins. Remember, if I can do it, you can do it.

With love and gratitude,

Ingrid

My pantry is a mishmash of American and Latin foods. Most of the recipes in this book call for common ingredients that you can find in your grocery store. As I travel throughout the country and discover new Latin markets and shops, I'll be adding their information to my website, so be sure to check in often for the latest and most updated list. The few minutes it will take you to seek out these unique ingredients will lead you to a whole new world of flavors and *delicioso* discoveries. For specialized Latin ingredients, like masa arepa, Latin cheeses, canned tropical fruits, chiles, and Latin seasonings, log onto my website, www.delicioso.com, for a list of my favorite food specialty shops, food catalogs, and online retailers.

the delicioso pantry

Here are the ingredients I consider indispensable:

cheese

■ **Cotija.** Also known as *queso añejado,* this aged white cheese is similar to feta, but drier and more crumbly. It comes in solid bricks or rounds and is great for sprinkling over corn, veggies, salads, and just about everything. Is there anything in this world that cheese is not good on?

■ **Oaxaca.** *¡Ay, qué rico*—how tasty! This cheese just melts in your mouth. It sometimes goes by the name *asadero.* Sold in discs or balls, it has a texture close to that of Monterey Jack or mozzarella. Try it in tortillas, tacos, and sandwiches.

■ **Queso blanco/queso fresco.** This creamy, mild, unripened cow's milk cheese is used in every Latin American country and is delish with tortillas, arepas, toast, and eggs. It's very soft and comes packed in tubs like cottage cheese. It is very widely available, but farmer cheese or fresh mozzarella would be good substitutes.

meats

■ **Chorizo.** This incredibly flavorful pork sausage is usually reddish in color. It is available fresh (uncooked), semi-cured, or cured, so read the package carefully before buying. Cured chorizo is very firm and is best eaten sliced, like pepperoni. Delicious when grilled, fresh chorizo can also be squeezed out of its casing and cooked until crumbly and browned. I love it both ways and use it in frittatas, in empanadas, and in my Tinga Poblana (page 159). Go for the preservative- and additive-free kind if you can find it.

■ **Serrano ham.** Similar to Italian prosciutto, Serrano ham is imported from Spain, where it is salt cured and air dried for six to eighteen months. It has a wonderful dense texture and a sweet nuttiness.

fruits

■ **Bitter orange.** The bitter orange (Seville orange) is commonly used in the mojos and marinades of Cuban cuisine. It is too sour to eat out of hand and has a rough, bruised appearance.

■ **Guanabana.** With a flavor somewhere between a pineapple, a banana, and a mango, the guanabana, also called a soursop, is one of the most enchanting tropical fruits. The

fruit itself has a spiky appearance and is oval or heart-shaped. The creamy juice is good in smoothies or cocktails.

■ **Guava.** This sweet, aromatic tropical fruit is believed to be native to southern Mexico or Central America. It bruises easily when ripe and is usually picked green. When it is fully ripe, the skin becomes soft and edible, and the interior, which is usually white, pink, yellow, or red, becomes sweet and creamy. Guava paste is excellent in sweet and savory recipes. I also use gorgeous magenta-colored Caribbean canned guava shells a lot. The pulp and seeds are removed and the shells are cooked in a sweet syrup. Smaller than a peach half, they are the perfect size for appetizer cups (the sweetness of guava is delicious with goat cheese) and make a really beautiful addition to a smoothie or a cocktail.

■ **Lime.** The two most common varieties of limes are the Persian (or Tahitian) and the Key lime, which is much smaller and less juicy than its larger cousin. I can't live without limes and I use them in everything.

■ **Lychee.** Wrapped in a bumpy raspberry-pink and leathery shell, the juicy lychee fruit is creamy white and incredibly sweet. Originally an Asian fruit, it is being grown more and more in tropical climates, including parts of Latin America. Lychees can be purchased fresh (discard the skin and black pit) or pitted and peeled, packed in syrup.

■ **Papaya.** Native to the Americas, papayas are about the size and shape of a football. If purchased green, a papaya should be left at room temperature for a couple of days (preferably in a brown paper bag) until it is bright orange-yellow or rose-colored (depending on the type of papaya) and ripe; once it is ripe, store it in the refrigerator. Slice in half and remove the seeds before eating. A bowl of papaya with fresh lime juice squeezed over it is my daily breakfast.

■ **Plantain.** The plantain looks like a large banana but is starchier and less sweet. More often than not, it is used for savory rather than sweet dishes. When it is unripe, the plantain's skin is green; when it is ripe, it turns yellow and then black. Though a fully ripened plantain might look rotten, the inside remains succulent and sweet and is less starchy than when green.

■ **Tomatillo.** Tomatillos look like small green tomatoes covered with a thin papery husk. They are tart and acidic and can be eaten raw or used in cooked sauces. Tomatillos are seen principally in Mexican cuisine.

herbs & seasonings

■ **Achiote.** Also known as annatto seed or bijol, achiote is used primarily to imbue food with a golden red color. It has a very muted musky flavor that quickly fades when achiote is combined with other seasonings. Achiote can be purchased in whole seed form or ground into a powder.

■ **Adobo.** Adobo is considered the backbone of most Latin cooking and is available as either a paste or a dry seasoning. It is used like salt and pepper, adding a distinct lemony garlic flavor to meats, soups, rice, beans, and vegetable dishes. You can purchase both forms of adobo at most supermarkets, but making it at home is more rewarding and allows you to control exactly what is going into it. Adobo typically includes chile powder, salt, vinegar, an assortment of herbs, cumin, garlic, citrus (either lime or bitter orange) and onions. See my recipe for adobo on page 22.

Chiles and ajis. See the chile glossary on page 20–21.

Cilantro. I use absurd amounts of cilantro in my cooking. No other herb is more commonly associated with Latin American cuisine than cilantro. It has a distinctive sweet and pungent aroma and a taste that people either love or hate. Cilantro is closely related to the carrot family and to parsley. The seeds of the cilantro plant are called coriander and are often used in cooking as well.

Culantro. Culantro is similar to cilantro in taste, but very different in appearance. It has long, narrow serrated leaves; is slightly more bitter than cilantro; and is most often used in salsas and sofritos (sautéed vegetables and herbs used as a base for soups, sauces, and bean and meat dishes). I love it in my Peruvian Chicken Soup (page 101). Although it is sometimes difficult to find in American supermarkets, it is becoming easier to source.

Cumin. Cumin seeds, either whole or ground, are used to flavor countless Latin American dishes. Cumin pairs well with and enhances meats but also complements many vegetables. Cumin seeds come from a small herb in the parsley family.

Lemongrass. This Asian stalk looks like a very long, woody scallion. Though the stalk is quite tough, its grassy-lemony essence can be infused into sauces and broths. Cut the thick base into 1 to 3-inch segments and bruise the stalk by smashing it with the back of a heavy knife before adding it to liquids or marinades.

Oregano. Oregano is most commonly associated with Mediterranean cuisine, but it is also used extensively in Central and South America. Cuban oregano is a succulent herb with a pungent flavor, while Mexican oregano has a strong, biting aroma and a sharp peppery flavor. The closest relative to oregano is marjoram.

Sugarcane. Though sugarcane is not native to the New World, when it was introduced to Latin America and the Caribbean it grew so well in the tropical climate that it soon became an important crop of that region. It's used as a sweetening agent and to produce rum, Brazilian cachaça, and several other spirits.

Tamarind. The sweet-sour pulp of tamarind pods is used in many parts of the world, including Latin America. Although one can buy the pods and soak them to extract the sour pulp, it is easier to buy seeded pulp in brick form or as

a paste. It is found in the Asian foods section of your supermarket or frozen as pulp in Latin markets.

---

vegetables

Chayote. This mild-flavored native Mexican squash is pale green and puckered on one end. It is used much like any other squash and can be roasted, boiled, or even stuffed.

Hearts of palm. Available fresh in some tropical regions and canned most everywhere else, hearts of palm are indeed the inner portion of a palm tree. They have a pleasantly mild flavor and look like the stalks of white asparagus.

Hominy. Sold in cans or dried, hominy is yellow or white corn kernels with the germ and hull removed. It can be added to stuffing and stews. In Peru, it's a traditional accompaniment to ceviche, as is canchita, which is dried and fried hominy kernels. Canchita is Peru's version of corn nuts and is yummy as a snack, even without ceviche.

Jicama. Jicama is most widely used in Mexican cuisine. The tan-skinned tuber has white flesh and a mild, sweet flavor but is mainly sought out for its light, crunchy texture, which is similar to that of a

▲ COTIJA ▼ CHORIZO   ▲ QUESO BLANCO   ▲ OAXACA ▼ BITTER ORANGE

▼ GUAVA   ▲ SERRANO HAM ▼ GUANABANA NECTAR   ▼ LYCHEES

▲ PAPAYAS

▲ PLANTAINS ▼ AJÍ PANCA

▲ TOMATILLOS

▲ ADOBO SPICES ▼ CHIPOTLES ▼ POBLANO PEPPER ▲ AJÍ AMARILLO ▼ SERRANO PEPPERS

water chestnut. It can be eaten raw or cooked and doesn't turn brown once cut, making it great for salads.

■ **Onions.** Many different kinds of onions are used in Latin cooking. *Red onions* are relatively sweet and mild with a soft edge and are most often used raw in salads and salsas. *Spanish onions* are sweeter and larger than yellow onions and are often used raw, especially when the color of a red onion is not desirable. *White onions* are common in Latin American dishes. They have a clean, tangy flavor and can be used interchangeably with Spanish onions. *Yellow onions* are considered too pungent to eat raw, but when cooked they develop a complex and sweet flavor. If in doubt, these onions work well in most cooked recipes.

■ **Potatoes.** Potatoes are native to Latin America and are an important part of the culture and the cuisine. While there are hundreds of varieties, the following are most commonly found in the United States. *Russets,* also called Idaho potatoes or baking potatoes, have a high starch and low moisture content and are good for roasting or French fries; versatile *Yukon Golds* are equally starchy and waxy and are a versatile potato suited to many applications like roasting, frying, or boiling; *red potatoes,* sometimes called creamers, are quite waxy and are great for potato salads; *purple potatoes* are delicious smashed or boiled; and *white boiling potatoes* are like Yukon Golds in their versatility.

■ **Scallions.** Also known as green onions, scallions have long green stalks and small white bulbs. Both the white and green parts can be used in recipes; most often the recipe will specify which part to use. They can be cooked or used raw.

■ **Shallots.** With a flavor between that of garlic and that of onion, shallots are wonderful cooked or raw in salads. Two large shallots can be used in place of one medium onion in most recipes.

■ **Yuca.** One of the most popular starchy, tropical tubers in Latin American cuisine, yuca (also called cassava or manioc) is used almost as frequently as the potato is in America. It has become even more convenient to use in recent years, as it can be found frozen in many supermarkets, sparing cooks the chore of peeling it and cutting it down to size. Its sweet though somewhat bland flavor lends itself well to being smothered in delicious sauces and deep-fried or baked to crisp perfection.

beans, grains, and seeds

■ **Beans.** Dozens of different beans and dried peas are used in Latin America, including black beans, red beans, lentils, chickpeas, black-eyed peas, fava beans, lima beans, pigeon peas, white beans, and pinto beans. They are an important source of protein and fiber and are eaten at nearly every meal.

■ **Pumpkin seeds (*pepitas*).** Hulled pumpkin seeds are used quite frequently in Mexican cuisine to add crunch and a nutty flavor. After the white shells are removed, the green seeds can be left raw or roasted and salted.

■ **Quinoa.** This ancient Andean grain has a light texture and a mild, nutty flavor that makes it an increasingly popular alternative to other grains. It is known as a "superfood" because it contains a balance of essential amino acids and a protein structure similar to that of milk.

■ **Rice.** Rice is a staple in most Latin American kitchens. Whether it is plain white rice, yellow rice, or an arroz con pollo, this popular grain almost always makes an appearance in Latin meals. Since the times of the Aztec empire, people have paired beans and rice, not only for a delicious, satisfying meal but because both foods together create a nourishing and complete protein.

flour and meal

■ **Cornmeal.** Cornmeal can be made in two ways: stone ground or water ground. Stone-ground cornmeal is popular because the process does not completely remove the hull and germ, making the meal more nutritious, though less shelf stable. Stone-ground cornmeal should be stored in the freezer and used within four months of opening the package. Water-ground cornmeal typically has all of the hull and germ removed. Of blue, white, and yellow cornmeals, yellow and blue are the sweetest.

■ **Masa arepa.** Masa arepa is precooked corn flour used to make arepas (see page 40). It is made from white or yellow corn flour and also goes by the names arepa masa, areparina, and masarepa. The brand available in the United States is masa harina P.A.N.

■ **Tapioca/yuca flour.** Because it is usually sold under the name tapioca starch, few people know that tapioca is a product of yuca. The key ingredient in many Latin American breads, such as Colombia's pan de yuca, yuca starch might be available in your supermarket or local Asian market.

canned or bottled goods

■ **Bottled sour orange.** If there are no sour or Seville oranges available at your market, this is an acceptable stand-in. You could also try mixing equal quantities of fresh orange juice and lime juice for a similar though not identical flavor.

■ **Dulce de leche.** Dulce de leche is known by several different names across the continent of South America: cajeta, arequipe, manjar. No matter what its name, this delicious treat of caramelized sweetened condensed milk can be used as a filling for cookies and cakes, as a dip for fruit, as a topping for ice cream, or as a spread for bread, crepes, and toast. I always have a few jars in my pantry.

■ **Evaporated milk.** Evaporated milk is regular milk from which 60 percent of the water content has been removed by way of evaporation. It comes in cans and keeps indefinitely. In many cuisines, evaporated milk becomes an important ingredient when fresh milk is not available. Evaporated milk is the key ingredient to creamy and flavorful textures in many Latin recipes.

■ **Maggi seasoning sauce.** Made from vegetable proteins and extracts, Maggi seasoning sauce is very much like Worcestershire sauce, and the two can be used interchangeably. I like to add it to marinades, stews, and sauces.

■ **Malta.** Though it is made with hops and barley, this carbonated malt beverage doesn't have any alcohol. It has a deep, molasses-like flavor and is a great alternative to chicken stock or beer for braised meats

■ **Sweetened condensed milk.** Condensed milk is a sweetened version of evaporated milk. It is also the base of homemade dulce de leche, which is made by boiling sweetened condensed milk in the unopened can for several hours. It's wonderful for mimicking the satiny texture of an egg custard when you don't have the time to make one from scratch!

▲LEMONGRASS ▼CHAYOTE   ▲SUGARCANE   ▲TAMARIND ▼JICAMA

▼HEARTS OF PALM   ▲HOMINY ▼YUCA   ▼GARBANZO BEANS

▲ BLACK BEANS   ▲ FAVA BEANS ▼ ASSORTED FLOURS   ▲ RED BEANS

▲ QUINOA ▼ DULCE DE LECHE   ▼ MALTA CARACAS   ▲ MASA CORNMEAL ▼ BITTER ORANGE JUICE

I consider myself a feisty *chica* who lives, works, and loves passionately. Whether this is due to genetics, to all the spicy chiles I eat, or to a combination of the two, I don't know, but I do know that life sure would be boring without spicy food! I use several kinds of chiles in my recipes: fresh, dried, canned in sauce, smoked, and powdered—each contributing its own special flavor. Not everything has to be mouth-tingling hot; sometimes just a hint of spice goes a long way. Although once in a while I love to spice food up to the point where it makes my nose run!

my spicy life

Typical fresh chiles like jalapeños and serranos often find their way into my sauces and salsas, but what I really love are Peruvian ají chiles, like ají amarillo, ají mirasol, and ají panca. The ají dates back thousands of years to the Incan culture, where it was a mythical character in poems and stories. Using these chiles makes me feel connected to these native Americans, and I like using authentic and typical South American ingredients as often as I can. In Miami, where I live, a large percentage of the population either is Latin or has Latin ancestry, so Latin ingredients are easy to find. For those of you who aren't lucky enough to have a Latin market on every corner, log onto my website (www.delicioso.com) for links to my favorite sources so you

can have a variety of chiles at your fingertips.

Fresh chiles can range from relatively mild, such as the poblano, to extremely hot, such as the Scotch bonnet. In general, the thicker the skin and the bigger the pepper, the milder it is, because up to 80 percent of the capsaicin (the compound that makes a chile spicy) is found in the seeds and ribs. Smaller chiles have more seeds and ribs in relation to flesh, making big bell peppers very mild, and teeny Scotch bonnets super hot! Removing the seeds and ribs from a chile makes it less spicy, but for the really hot ones, not even this will provide much relief.

I encourage you to wear latex or kitchen gloves when handling spicy chiles, because even touching a chile's seeds or ribs can lead to an uncomfortable burning sensation if you accidentally touch a sensitive part of your face or rub your eyes. The potent capsaicin oils can actually stay active on your hands even after you rinse them, so do handle these chiles with care.

When I don't want to deal with gloves, seeds, and ribs, I cut off the bottom portion of the chile, using only the part beneath where the seeds begin. This way my hands never go near the seeds or the ribs. Just remember to remove the piece of chile before serving, otherwise one person will be rewarded with a mouthful of fire!

■ **Ají amarillo.** Used in Peruvian cuisine for thousands of years, the ají amarillo is a 4- to 6-inch-long tapered yellow chile that is moderately hot (like a jalapeño) and slightly fruity. I use these chiles mostly canned in brine, dried, or as a paste, but in South America they are readily available fresh.

■ **Ají mirasol.** This pepper's name means "looking at the sun," a reference to how the chile grows. It's a moderate to very hot chile that is usually a deep yellowish red. It tastes tropical and berry-like and is widely used in its dried and powdered form in South America, particularly in Peruvian cuisine.

■ **Ají panca.** This dried chile has a smoky berry-like flavor and is mostly used in sauces and fish-based dishes. Archaeological evidence suggests that it was used up to 6,500 years ago. A common Peruvian chile, it has thick flesh with a moderate yet lasting semi-hot spice.

■ **Cayenne pepper.** When fresh, cayenne peppers are 2½ inches long; however, this red chile is most commonly used dried and ground into a fine powder. Cayenne is pungent, tart, and smoky and is a good seasoning for almost everything.

■ **Habanero.** Native to the Caribbean, the Yucatán, and the coastal northern region of South America, the habanero is known as one of the hottest little peppers. It varies from green to bright orange and is related to Scotch bonnets. Adding just a sliver of the spicy chile can turn a sauce or stew into liquid fire!

■ **Jalapeño.** The jalapeño has become one of the most common and recognizable chiles in the United States. Its heat runs the gamut from moderately spicy to pretty spicy. The jalapeño is eaten raw in salsas and cooked sauces. Its color is most often deep to medium green, but it can lighten to orangey-red when ripe. Ripe jalapeños are also smoke-dried to make *chipotle chiles.* These are quite flavorful, especially when packed in adobo, a sauce made of tomatoes, vinegar, and spices. Canned *chipotle chiles en adobo* are quite spicy, so be sure to remove the seeds before using if you're spice-sensitive.

■ **Poblano.** Low to moderate in heat, poblanos are always served cooked, never raw. This is a good pepper for roasting and great for stuffing because of its relatively thick skin and large size. *Ancho chiles,* the dried version of poblanos, are the main ingredient in Mexican mole sauces. This is a mild dried chile with a very complex flavor, and is the most widely used dry chile in Mexico.

■ **Scotch bonnet.** This is one of the hottest chiles around. Its flavor is fruity and smoky, and it is widely used in Caribbean fare, such as jerk chicken.

■ **Serrano.** Hot and acidic, serranos are for those who are ready to graduate from milder jalapeños. Red serranos can be a bit sweeter, but the degree of heat varies. These small chiles can be used fresh, cooked in sauce, or pickled. They're thin and long with a pointed end. Dried serranos are called *chile seco.*

living *la vida* saucy

These are my versions of a few classic sauces and seasonings from the Latin kitchen. They can make the flavor of a chicken breast, a pork chop, or a steak really pop, and they add a kick to even the plainest rice-and-bean dinner. Adobo and sofrito are the heart and soul of many Latin dishes. There are many variations, but these are the ones that I like best. You can build a sauce or a stew from them or use them as a finishing touch for fish or meat. I make salsa mole when I want something rich and intensely flavorful but don't have more than a few minutes to put it together. With some prepared mole paste, you can make a pretty authentic version in minutes. The jalapeño salsa and the avocado ají are the kinds of piquant condiments that you find on the table in most any Latin home. Try them instead of ketchup or a tomato-based salsa for something a little different and insanely tasty with dinner.

delicioso adobo seasoning

MAKES ⅓ CUP

Adobo seasoning is wonderful on everything. It adds a kick to soups and sauce and is great as a spice rub or mixed with liquids for a marinade. You can buy it bottled (see "The Delicioso Pantry," page 10) or make the homemade version here to keep in your own pantry. Store it in a tightly covered glass jar in a dark, dry, cool spot (the cabinet above your stove is the worst place to store spices!). It will keep for up to six months.

- 1 tablespoon lemon-pepper seasoning
- 1 tablespoon garlic powder
- 1 tablespoon onion powder or flakes
- 1 tablespoon dried oregano
- 1 tablespoon parsley flakes
- 1 tablespoon achiote powder
- 1½ teaspoons ground cumin
- 1 tablespoon salt

Combine the spices in a small glass jar and seal with an airtight lid. Shake to blend and store in a cool, dry place.

salsa mole

MAKES 4 CUPS

Mole is a sauce typical of Mexico, but there's nothing typical about mole. It can be made from pumpkin seeds, sesame seeds, a number of different kinds of chiles, and even chocolate (yes, chocolate!). It's absolutely brilliant over chicken or with turkey but is also wonderful with beans and rice. It is famously complicated to make, but when you rely on prepared mole paste as your base, it's a snap to put together. You can find mole paste in most supermarkets, or see "The Delicioso Pantry," page 10.

- 1 teaspoon unsalted butter or olive oil
- 1 small yellow onion, finely chopped
- 1 small tomato, cored and finely chopped
- 4 garlic cloves, finely chopped
- 2 cups prepared black, green, or red mole paste
- 1 to 2 cups homemade or canned
  low-sodium chicken broth
- Salt and freshly ground pepper

Melt the butter or heat the oil in a medium saucepan over medium-high heat. Add the onion, tomato, and garlic and cook, stirring often, until the onion is soft and starting to brown, 5 to 7 minutes. Stir in the mole paste and add enough chicken broth to make it as thick (like pancake batter) or thin (like cream sauce) as you like. Add some salt and pepper, heat the sauce through, and serve.

avocado ají

MAKES 1/3 CUP

If I had a dollar for every ají in the world, I'd be a very rich *chica*! This one goes with just about anything, from grilled beef or chicken to yucca, chorizo, potatoes, and rice.

    8 scallions, white and light green parts only,
        finely chopped
    2 medium tomatoes, cored and finely chopped
    1½ cups finely chopped fresh cilantro leaves
    ¼ cup white vinegar
    Salt
    2 medium Hass avocados, halved, pitted
        peeled, and chopped into small cubes
    2 hard-boiled eggs, peeled and chopped
    Tabasco sauce
    1 lime, cut into wedges

Place the scallions, tomatoes, cilantro, vinegar, ½ cup of water, and some salt in a large bowl and stir to combine. Add the avocados, eggs, and a few dashes of Tabasco and stir gently to combine, being careful not to mash the avocados or eggs too much. Cover with plastic wrap and refrigerate until chilled. Serve within a couple of hours, garnished with lime wedges.

basic sofrito

MAKES 1½ CUPS

With sofrito in your fridge, you will never eat another bland or boring meal again! Sofrito adds instant oomph to everything from beans and lentils to chicken, beef, and potatoes. You can use it as a base for soups or as a topping for broiled chicken breasts or pork chops. It keeps for up to a week in an airtight container—or freeze it in an ice cube tray and use the cubes like bouillon, adding a hit of flavor whenever you need it. For a spicy sofrito, add a chopped jalapeño.

    2 tablespoons unsalted butter or olive oil
    12 scallions, white and light green parts only,
        finely chopped
    1 small yellow onion, finely chopped
    1 small tomato, cored and chopped
    ¼ cup chopped cilantro leaves
    Salt and freshly ground pepper

Melt the butter or heat the oil in a medium skillet over medium heat. Add the remaining ingredients and cook, stirring often, until the onion is soft and golden and the tomato is broken down and pasty, about 10 minutes. Transfer to a bowl and set aside to cool, or use immediately.

jalapeño salsa

MAKES 1 CUP

Walk into a Mexican home and you will see something like this sauce on the table. It's used as a condiment to add zing to absolutely anything and everything. This version is light and intensely flavorful.

    ½ cup sliced pickled jalapeños, drained
        and finely chopped
    ½ small yellow onion, finely chopped
    ½ cup finely chopped fresh cilantro leaves
    2 tablespoons olive oil
    1 tablespoon white vinegar
    1 tablespoon lime juice (from about ½ lime)
    Salt

Combine all of the ingredients in a medium bowl and mix together. Let the salsa sit at room temperature for a few hours for the flavors to come together, or refrigerate in an airtight container for up to 1 week.

pillow talk

I miss the carefree days of childhood when I would fill up on a giant, homemade breakfast and then go back to bed. What a luxury! At this point in my life, those days are a distant memory. Breakfast is the power fuel we burn throughout the day—a good reason not to skip it.

On busy weekday mornings, I'm usually happy with a bowl of chopped papaya sprinkled with lime juice or leftovers from dinner the night before, but weekends are about treating myself with the comfort foods I grew up with, such as fresh-griddled arepas, hot-from-the-oven pan de yuca, and my sister's famous quiche. Sometimes I'll make something really traditional, like herby changua broth with poached eggs or avena, an oatmeal breakfast smoothie that is completely satisfying and wonderful. Other times I'll make something that's a mix of my past and my present, like Plantain Bread (page 36), Tutti Frutti Toast with Dulce de Leche (page 31), or Eggs Benedict with Chipotle Hollandaise (page 32).

As a good Latin girl, I sometimes start my day off with a steak, and in this chapter, my gift to you is the absolute best version of steak and eggs, called Bistec a Caballo, "Steak on Horseback." This is how I grew up eating steak and eggs, and my mother would have my head if I prepared it any other way (though there are different, equally enticing versions throughout Latin America). Follow Bistec a Caballo with a cortadito, espresso–style coffee, and you'll have enough energy for today and tomorrow.

Sweet or savory, pick your glory—you'll find both in this chapter. *¡Buenos días!*

homey changua breakfast broth

SERVES 4

1 tablespoon white vinegar

4 large eggs

1½ cups milk

3 scallions, light green and white parts only, thinly sliced

2 tablespoons chopped fresh cilantro leaves

¼ teaspoon salt

Rustic country bread or toast, for serving

Legend has it that Simón Bolívar, *el Libertador* of Latin and South America, fed this broth to his troops while emancipating the people of Bolivia, Colombia, Ecuador, Panama, Peru, and Venezuela. Everyone, even highbrow Colombians, eats changua and feels the better for it. Use rustic country bread or toast to break up the egg and soak up the delicious broth.

1 Fill a large saucepan with 2 inches of cold water. Add the vinegar and bring the liquid to a simmer over medium-high heat. Reduce the heat to medium. One at a time, crack the eggs into a small cup or ramekin and gently slide them into the hot water. Poach the eggs until the whites are set but the yolks are still runny, 2 to 3 minutes. Using a slotted spoon, transfer the eggs to 4 bowls and set aside.

2 Bring 4 cups of water and the milk to a boil in a medium saucepan over medium-high heat. Reduce the heat to medium low, add the scallions, cilantro, and salt, and simmer for 5 minutes. Ladle the broth over the eggs and serve immediately with bread or toast.

old-fashioned avena oatmeal
breakfast smoothies

SERVES 4

1 cup old-fashioned oatmeal

6 cups milk, plus more if needed

2 tablespoons to ¼ cup sugar

Pinch of cinnamon

1 teaspoon vanilla extract (optional)

Avena means "oats." This is a thick breakfast drink made with oatmeal, similar in texture to a smoothie. Yucca buns (Pan de Yuca, page 34) are the traditional partner to this breakfast or afternoon snack. The best avena smoothies and pan de yuca are to be found in Colombia at a little place in Bogotá called Fru Fru or at El Espinal in the town plaza of Girardot, two hours from Bogotá on the Magdalena River. I don't get to Colombia often anymore, so I make myself an avena smoothie whenever I long for a taste of home. For a thinner version, strain the oat mixture before refrigerating.

1 Place the oatmeal and milk in a medium saucepan over medium-high heat and bring to a rapid simmer. Reduce the heat to medium low and cook, stirring constantly, until the oatmeal is thick, about 10 minutes. Add sugar and cinnamon to taste and set the oatmeal aside to cool slightly.

2 Transfer the oatmeal to a container and refrigerate for at least 2 hours or overnight. Strain the liquid, add the vanilla (if using), and add more milk if you want it thinner. Serve cold.

huevos rancheros with salsa ranchera

SERVES 4

FOR THE SALSA

2½ pounds tomatoes, cored and halved

1 to 2 fresh or pickled serrano chiles, halved (seeded and ribbed for less heat)

1 tablespoon olive oil

½ small yellow onion, finely chopped

2 garlic cloves, finely minced

1 teaspoon chopped fresh oregano leaves

½ teaspoon ground cumin

1 teaspoon Worcestershire sauce

Salt and freshly ground pepper

FOR THE EGGS

2 tablespoons unsalted butter

8 large eggs

Salt and freshly ground pepper

4 yellow corn tortillas or tostadas

12 scallions, light green parts only, chopped

¼ cup chopped fresh cilantro leaves

A former boyfriend who grew up in Mexico turned me on to the wonders of Mexican food. When I visited him in Mexico, we'd always have huevos rancheros for breakfast. This is just the kind of home-style food that I love.

1 To make the salsa, preheat your broiler to high. Arrange the tomatoes on an aluminum-foil-lined broiler pan skin side up. Broil until their skins start to char and shrivel, about 3 minutes. Turn the tomatoes over and broil for an additional 10 to 12 minutes, or until they are soft. Transfer the tomatoes and the chiles to a blender, purée, and set aside.

2 Heat the olive oil in a medium saucepan over medium-high heat for 1 minute. Add the onion and the garlic and cook, stirring occasionally, until the onion is soft, about 2 minutes. Stir in the oregano, cumin, and Worcestershire sauce. Add the tomato purée and simmer until the sauce is slightly thickened and the flavors have blended, about 10 minutes. Season with some salt and pepper and set aside.

3 To make the eggs, melt the butter in a large skillet over medium heat. Carefully crack the eggs into the pan, season with some salt and pepper, cover, and cook until the whites are cooked through but the yolks are still runny, 6 to 8 minutes. Meanwhile, heat a small skillet over medium-high heat. Add a tortilla and warm on each side for 10 to 15 seconds, or until it's heated through. Serve 2 fried eggs on each tortilla, topped with warm salsa ranchera and sprinkled with scallions and cilantro.

chica tip: Store your eggs upside down, with the wider end pointing up. This way the egg's natural air sac remains on top, keeping your eggs fresher longer.

tutti frutti toast with dulce de leche

SERVES 4

4 1-inch-thick slices of brioche, egg bread, or white country bread

1 cup blueberries, plus extra for serving

1 cup chopped strawberries, plus extra for serving

4 large eggs

½ cup milk, plus extra if needed

1 teaspoon vanilla extract

Pinch of salt

2 tablespoons unsalted butter

1 cup dulce de leche, at room temperature

Confectioners' sugar, for serving

Here is a great example of what happens to a Latina after she's lived in America for twenty years. One morning when I was making French toast, I decided to substitute dulce de leche for the maple syrup, and it was so delicious that I swore I would never use maple syrup again. For the best French toast, use a loaf of brioche or egg bread, such as challah. You can find dulce de leche in many supermarkets and most Latin markets, or see "The Delicioso Pantry," page 10.

1 Place the bread on a cutting board and use a long, sharp knife to cut a pocket horizontally into each slice.

2 Place the blueberries and strawberries in a small bowl and gently combine. Fill each bread pocket with a tablespoon of the berry mixture. Press down gently with the palm of your hand to flatten the bulge in the bread slightly.

3 Beat the eggs, 2 tablespoons of the milk, the vanilla, and salt together in a medium bowl. Dip each piece of stuffed bread into the egg mixture, allowing the bread to become saturated on both sides, and place them on a plate.

4 Melt the butter in a large skillet or griddle over medium heat. Add the French toasts and cook until golden on both sides, about 3 minutes per side.

5 While the toasts brown, bring a small saucepan of water to a simmer over medium-high heat. Place the dulce de leche and the remaining 2 tablespoons of milk in a heat-proof bowl and set it over the saucepan. Reduce the heat to low and whisk until the sauce is smooth and pourable, adding more milk if necessary.

6 Drizzle the French toast with the dulce de leche sauce. Top with a few more berries and sprinkle with confectioners' sugar.

eggs benedict with chipotle hollandaise

SERVES 4

FOR THE CHIPOTLE HOLLANDAISE

½ cup (1 stick) unsalted butter

3 large egg yolks

2 tablespoons hot water

1 tablespoon plus 1 teaspoon fresh lemon juice

⅛ teaspoon salt

1 tablespoon sauce from a can of chipotles en adobo

FOR THE EGGS

2 tablespoons white vinegar

4 large eggs

1½ teaspoons dried oregano

½ teaspoon paprika

4 slices Canadian bacon

4 store-bought white corn arepas, English muffins, or pieces of bread

Chopped fresh flat-leaf parsley leaves, for serving

Chipotle chiles en adobo are one of my favorite ingredients; they add a smoky, spicy flavor to absolutely anything, from pasta and beans to stew and rice. A little bit goes a long way, though, so when I open a can I like to make little single-use packets with the guaranteed leftovers. I place one chipotle with some sauce on a sheet of plastic wrap, fold it into a neat square, and freeze it on a baking sheet. When the packets are frozen solid, I store them in a freezer bag, so they're ready for action whenever I am.

If you're not up to making arepas from scratch and can't find them in your grocery store, use toasted English muffin halves instead.

1 Make the hollandaise first. Melt the butter in a small saucepan over medium-low heat until it is foamy but not browned, about 5 minutes. Bring a small saucepan of water to a boil. Reduce the heat to medium low and set a small bowl on top of the saucepan (the bottom of the bowl should not touch the water). Add the egg yolks, hot water, lemon juice, salt, and adobo sauce to the bowl and whisk until foamy and just starting to thicken, about 5 minutes.

2 Add the melted butter and whisk the sauce until it is smooth. Turn off the heat and cover the bowl with plastic wrap. Let the sauce stand over the warm water for up to 30 minutes before serving. (If the sauce thickens too much or starts to separate, whisk in hot water a teaspoon at a time until it comes back together or thins out. Don't reheat the sauce over direct heat in a saucepan; it will separate.)

3 To make the eggs, fill a large saucepan with 2 inches of cold water. Add the vinegar and bring the liquid to a simmer over medium-high heat. Reduce the heat to medium. One at a time, crack the eggs into a small cup or ramekin and gently slide them into the skillet. Poach the eggs until the whites are set but the yolks are still runny, 2 to 3 minutes. Using a slotted spoon, transfer the eggs to a paper-towel-lined plate to drain.

4 Combine the oregano and paprika in a small bowl and rub the mixture onto the Canadian bacon. Heat a medium nonstick skillet over medium heat and add the bacon slices. Cook until their edges begin to turn golden brown, about 3 minutes on each side.

5 Warm the arepas in a large skillet over medium-high heat for 10 to 15 seconds on each side, or until they're heated through. If using English muffins or bread, toast until they're golden brown.

6 To assemble, place a warm arepa on each serving plate. Top with a slice of the Canadian bacon and a poached egg. Spoon some of the chipotle hollandaise over the egg and sprinkle with the chopped parsley. Serve immediately.

chica tip: For perfectly poached eggs, use a whisk to create a small whirlpool in the simmering water. Slide the egg into the center of the whirlpool while whisking (whisk around the egg—don't whisk the egg itself) so the egg whites don't disperse. The water must not be boiling too briskly or the egg will disintegrate.

yuca buns (pan de yuca)

MAKES 10 BUNS

1 cup tapioca flour, plus extra for kneading

1 teaspoon baking powder

2 cups finely grated Oaxaca cheese or other fresh white cheese, such as mozzarella

2 large egg yolks

¼ cup heavy cream, if needed

Be forewarned, these are addictive: Once you start eating them, you just can't stop! I used to make them as dinner rolls for parties, but I gave it up when my guests would fill up on the rolls, leaving no room for all the food I made.

1 Preheat your oven to 350°F. Line a baking sheet with aluminum foil, grease the foil with vegetable oil cooking spray, and set aside.

2 Whisk the tapioca flour and baking powder together in a large bowl. Stir in the cheese and egg yolks. Once the dough forms a ball, turn it out onto a lightly floured board and knead it with your hands until the dough is smooth, evenly textured, and not sticky. If the dough doesn't come together or seems too stiff to knead, then add cream, 1 tablespoon at a time, until it comes together and is supple.

3 Divide the dough into 10 even pieces and shape them into little crescents or balls. Place them 1 inch apart on the prepared baking sheet and bake until the rolls are pale gold (not browned), 15 to 17 minutes (they will still be tender and soft). Cool on a wire rack for 5 to 10 minutes and serve while still warm.

joha's cheesy quiche

SERVES 4

2 tablespoons olive oil

1 cup diced ham (preferably Serrano)

8 scallions, light green parts only, thinly sliced

1 14-ounce can diced tomatoes, drained

3 large eggs

1 cup grated Gouda cheese

½ cup milk

¼ cup heavy cream

¼ cup sliced kalamata olives

1 tablespoon drained brine-packed capers

Freshly ground pepper

1 premade 9-inch pie shell

My older sister, Johanna, loves food and cooking as much as I do. When I was young, she would bribe me with food to keep my mouth shut about her misadventures. Now she lives in Toronto, and we spend countless hours on the phone confessing our food indulgences and recipe successes and failures. We both love breakfast for dinner, and her cheesy quiche tastes equally yummy for either.

1 Preheat your oven to 350°F.

2 Heat the oil in a medium skillet over medium-high heat. Add the ham and scallions and cook until browned, 3 to 5 minutes. Stir in the tomatoes and cook until they are reduced to a jammy texture, 5 to 8 minutes. Set the mixture aside to cool.

3 Whisk the eggs, cheese, milk, cream, olives, and capers, and pepper together in a medium bowl. Stir the tomato mixture into the eggs and pour it into the pie shell. Bake the quiche until the eggs are set, 30 to 35 minutes. Place the quiche on a wire rack to cool for 40 minutes before serving, or serve at room temperature.

plantain bread

MAKES 3 MINI LOAVES

½ cup (1 stick) plus 1½ tablespoons unsalted butter, at room temperature

2 cups all-purpose flour

1 teaspoon baking soda

¼ teaspoon salt

1 cup sugar

2 large eggs, lightly beaten

2 ripe plantains, peeled, coarsely chopped, and lightly mashed

1 banana, peeled, coarsely chopped, and lightly mashed

⅓ cup buttermilk

Less sweet than traditional banana bread, plantain bread is excellent for breakfast, with tea, or as an afternoon snack. I make it in giant batches and wrap individual loaves as gifts for friends. The loaves also make a sweet present for dinner guests to take home with them; that way they'll think about how much fun they had and how thoughtful you are when they unwrap the plantain bread in the morning. Serve the bread toasted, spread generously with butter and drizzled with honey.

1 Preheat your oven to 350°F. Grease 3 mini loaf pans with the 1½ tablespoons of butter and set aside.

2 Sift the flour, baking soda, and salt into a medium bowl and set aside.

3 Using an electric mixer, cream the ½ cup butter and the sugar in a medium bowl until it is pale and light, about 3 minutes. Gradually add the eggs a little at a time, beating until they're completely incorporated. Add the plantains and banana, mashing them into the batter with a fork. With the mixer on low speed, add half of the sifted dry ingredients, mixing until just a few dry patches remain. Add the buttermilk and then the remaining dry ingredients, mixing until just combined.

4 Transfer the batter to the greased mini loaf pans. Bake until the tops are golden and a toothpick inserted in the center comes out clean, about 40 minutes. Cool the loaves for 10 minutes before turning them out onto a wire rack to cool completely.

frittata antioquena

SERVES 6

2 teaspoons canola or vegetable oil

2 cooked chorizo sausages, finely chopped

2 slices of white bread, crusts removed

1 ripe black-skinned plantain, peeled and finely chopped

6 large eggs

Salt and freshly ground pepper

1 tablespoon unsalted butter

chica tip: If your frittata splits as you're sliding it out of the skillet, serve it folded like an omelet or stack it in roughly torn "rustic" wedges. Just like that, you're chic instead of clumsy!

I used to always make a hearty egg tortilla, the Spanish version of a frittata, for breakfast before going horseback riding with friends on a daylong *cabalgata* in the countryside. We'd sing songs, laugh, and drink lots of *aguardiente*, a super-powerful anise-flavored "fire water" made from sugar-cane. Frittatas are perfect for picnics or brunches because you can make them ahead of time and serve them at room temperature. Sweet plantains add a wonderful richness that is really yummy with the spicy chorizo.

1 Heat 1 teaspoon of the oil in a large skillet over medium-high heat. Add the chorizo and brown, stirring often, until completely heated through, about 4 minutes. Transfer to a paper-towel-lined plate and set aside.

2 Toast the bread slices until golden brown, then cut each slice into ½-inch croutons and set aside.

3 Heat the remaining teaspoon of oil in a large skillet over medium-high heat. Add the chopped plantain and cook, stirring often, until browned, 3 to 4 minutes. Transfer the plantain to a paper-towel-lined plate.

4 Whisk the eggs with salt and pepper to taste in a large bowl. Add the plantain and croutons and gently stir to incorporate. Melt the butter in a large nonstick skillet over medium heat. Add the egg mixture, tilting the pan so that the eggs spread out into a thin layer. Once you see the eggs starting to set around the edges, reduce the heat to low and add the chorizo. Cover the skillet and cook the frittata until it's completely cooked through, about 10 minutes. Carefully slide the frittata onto a serving dish, slice into wedges, and serve.

steak on horseback (bistec a caballo)

SERVES 4

4½ teaspoons olive oil

2 medium tomatoes, cored and chopped

4 scallions, white and light green parts only, halved lengthwise and cut crosswise into 1-inch-long strips

1 garlic clove, finely minced

Salt and freshly ground pepper

2 tablespoons unsalted butter

1½ pounds skirt or hanger steak, cut crosswise into 4 pieces

1 teaspoon Delicioso Adobo Seasoning (page 22) or purchased adobo

4 large eggs

2 tablespoons chopped fresh flat-leaf parsley

I don't know a meat-eating man on earth who wouldn't be thrilled to see Bistec a Caballo on the breakfast table. Unlike your standard steak-and-egg fare, it comes with a hot salsa, made from quickly seared tomatoes, scallions, and garlic. It adds a wonderful complexity to this otherwise straight-shooting dish. If you need to patch things up with your significant other, Steak on Horseback first thing the next morning beats a dozen roses or tickets to a basketball game anytime!

1 Heat 1½ teaspoons of the olive oil in a medium skillet over medium-high heat. Add the tomatoes, scallions, and garlic, cook until the scallions are softened, about 3 minutes, and then season with salt and pepper to taste. Turn the heat down as low as possible to keep the sauce warm and stir occasionally while you make the steak and eggs.

2 Heat the remaining 3 teaspoons of olive oil with 1 tablespoon of the butter in a large skillet over medium-high heat. Season the steaks with the adobo and sear them in the skillet until they are browned on both sides but still pink in the middle, 2 to 3 minutes per side (a little longer if you prefer a well-done steak). Transfer them to individual plates and set aside.

3 Melt the remaining tablespoon of butter in the same skillet and add the eggs, frying them until the whites are fully cooked but the yolks are still runny, about 4 minutes. Top each steak with some tomato sauce and then gently place an egg on top. Sprinkle with chopped parsley and serve.

yellow corn arepas (arepas de choclo)

MAKES APPROXIMATELY 16 AREPAS

1 16-ounce bag frozen corn kernels or 2 cups fresh kernels sliced from the cob

1 cup milk

2 tablespoons sugar

¾ teaspoon salt

Freshly ground pepper

2 cups fine yellow cornmeal

4 tablespoons (½ stick) unsalted butter

Yellow corn arepas are sweeter than plain white cornmeal arepas. They're excellent for breakfast with a café con leche or as an afternoon snack with some cheese. When I feel like treating myself, I sandwich two small slices of Oaxaca cheese (or other fresh, soft melting cheese) between two arepas and toast them in a skillet until the cheese melts. Sinful! For cute bite-size arepas, use 2 tablespoons of batter to make an arepa about 2 inches in diameter. For a family-size arepa, use ¼ cup of batter and then slice the arepa into quarters when it's finished cooking.

1 Defrost the corn by placing it in a colander and rinsing it under cold water. Drain well and set aside for about 10 minutes.

2 Place the defrosted corn in a blender and purée it with the milk, sugar, salt, and pepper to taste. Transfer the mixture to a medium bowl and stir in the cornmeal to make a pancake-like batter.

3 Melt 2 tablespoons of the butter in a large nonstick skillet or griddle over medium-high heat. Add 3 tablespoons of the arepa batter and use the bottom of a spoon to flatten and spread the batter into a 3- to 4-inch circle. Fry 2 to 4 arepas at a time until they are golden brown and crisp on both sides, 8 to 10 minutes total. Add more butter from the remaining 2 tablespoons to the skillet between batches when necessary.

all about arepas

Arepas are a very typical food in many Latin American countries. In their most basic form they are made simply from masa arepa, which is lime-treated corn flour, water, and salt. Although they are very easy to make at home, arepas are becoming more and more popular in the United States and can often be found in the refrigerated section (with the tortillas) or in the freezer aisle of many supermarkets. Store-bought arepas are fully cooked and only require heating in the oven or a skillet before eating. You can even deep-fry them, as they do on Colombia's coast. Crunchy and sweet, they're *¡muy delicioso!*

Arepas are used differently depending on who is eating them. Venezuelans turn them into sandwiches stuffed with *reina pepiada* (Venezuelan chicken salad) or spiced, shredded meat, while Colombians eat them with a meal (in place of tortillas) or slathered with butter or soft farmer cheese for breakfast. I don't discriminate; I like mine all ways, from the thin and crispy Arepa Chips (page 56) common in Bogotá to arepas con queso and the rich, sweet Arepas de Choclo (page 40) made with corn and often stuffed with Oaxaca cheese. Yucca arepas are quite tasty, too; they're made with yucca flour instead of corn flour and have a delicious, though very different, flavor.

appeteasers and little snacks

I try to approach every meal as if it is a celebration, and the recipes in this chapter are some of my favorite happy foods. I count on these quick recipes for easy snacks and nibbles to bring a festive feeling into my home absolutely every day, whether I am making a quick snack or throwing a full-scale fiesta. Based mostly on traditional Latin snacks called *bocados,* these small dishes can serve to sate or tease your appetite.

To arrange a truly *fabuloso* affair, you've got to have great food. Bright-colored, fun, and tasty appetizers get any gathering going, and nothing breaks the ice at a party better than a spread of really delicious finger foods. Big, bold flavors set an upbeat mood and are conversation starters. Don't think everything has to be fancy; who has time to make everything from scratch? Olives and roasted nuts are delish paired with Chorizo Empanadas (page 58), and Ham and Cheese Croquetas (page 49) make a platter of store-bought cheese and Stuffed Mushrooms (page 55) look like a feast. These are the kinds of *delicioso* bites made for one-handed nibbling; you should always be able to balance a snack in one hand and a cocktail in the other gracefully!

I've been known to throw a party for absolutely any occasion and for no reason at all. Who says you need a reason to get friends together for a good time, anyway? Nothing gives me more pleasure than gathering with friends and loved ones to eat and drink and celebrate. Whether it's coffee and a snack with a girlfriend or drinks with lots of friends, the festive foods on the following pages make any get-together an instant special occasion.

shrimp cocktail salad (vuelve a la vida)

SERVES 4 TO 6

Juice of 5 limes

¾ cup ketchup

1 teaspoon Worcestershire sauce

½ cup water or dry white wine, as needed

4 cups small cooked shrimp

½ medium yellow onion, finely chopped

2 medium Hass avocados, halved, pitted, peeled, and chopped

Hot sauce

Salt and freshly ground pepper

3 tablespoons chopped fresh cilantro leaves, for serving

Toasted bread or crackers

Vuelve a la vida means "back to life" and is the name for this traditional Mexican recipe, which is a cross between a shrimp salad and a shrimp cocktail. You can serve it with another type of cracker, petite toast, or crostini, but I love it with Saltines.

1 Stir the lime juice, ketchup, and Worcestershire sauce together in a large bowl. If the mixture seems thick, add the water or wine to dilute the sauce. Add the shrimp, onion, and avocados and toss to coat. Season with your favorite hot sauce and stir in salt and pepper to taste.

2 Cover with plastic wrap and refrigerate until you are ready to serve. Sprinkle with the chopped cilantro and serve on toasted bread or with some crackers on the side.

black bean dip

SERVES 4 TO 6

2 tablespoons olive oil

1 medium yellow onion, chopped

2 garlic cloves, chopped

2 15-ounce cans black beans, rinsed and drained

½ teaspoon ground cumin

Red pepper flakes (optional)

Salt

1 6-ounce container plain yogurt

2 large tomatoes, halved, cored, seeded, and finely diced

½ cup chopped fresh cilantro leaves, for serving

This dip is head and shoulders above the bland stuff that comes in a can. You can serve it in a bowl surrounded by chips or sliced jicama, or spread it on toasted bread for black bean bruschetta. It's so easy to make that you'll find yourself turning to it time and again. I've also found it freezes well, making it a perfect "emergency" appetizer to offer unexpected company.

1 Heat the olive oil in a large skillet over medium-high heat for 1 minute. Add the onion and garlic and cook, stirring occasionally, until the onion is soft, about 2 minutes. Scrape the onion mixture into a blender or a food processor along with the drained beans, the cumin, red pepper flakes, and salt, scraping down the sides of the blender jar or food processor as necessary. (If the purée is very thick, add 1 to 2 tablespoons of water or chicken broth to help the blending process and make the purée smoother.)

2 Transfer the purée to a bowl and fold in the yogurt and diced tomatoes. Serve immediately or cover with plastic wrap and refrigerate for up to 3 days (let the dip return to room temperature before serving). Sprinkle with the chopped cilantro just before serving.

chica tip: Freeze leftover bean dip in half-cup portions in a quart-size resealable freezer bag. Defrost one portion and heat it with some chicken broth or water and you have instant soup!

simple spanish tortilla

SERVES 4 TO 6

½ cup olive oil

4 large Yukon Gold potatoes, peeled and sliced about ⅛ inch thick

½ large yellow onion, chopped

6 large eggs

¼ cup milk

Salt and freshly ground pepper

Chopped fresh flat-leaf parsley, for garnish

chica tip: Spanish tortillas are great for picnics and parties because they don't need reheating before serving. Save yourself half the prep time by using frozen cooked sliced or shredded potatoes instead of raw ones.

Spanish tortillas are basically omelets made with potatoes. In Spain it's called a *tortilla de patatas* or *tortilla Española* and is served any time of day alone, or as part of a tapas spread. Don't confuse these with Mexican flatbread tortillas—they couldn't be more different!

1 Heat the olive oil in a 10-inch skillet over medium-high heat for 1 minute. Reduce the heat to medium and add the potato slices a few at a time so they don't stick together. Add the onion and cook, stirring occasionally, until the potatoes are tender and the onion is golden but not brown, about 10 minutes. Place a strainer over a bowl in your sink and transfer the potato and onion mixture to it to drain; reserve the oil.

2 Whisk the eggs, milk, add some salt and pepper together in a large bowl. Add the potatoes and onions to the egg mixture and combine until they are completely mixed in. Set the bowl aside for about 15 minutes to let the potatoes release some of their starches into the eggs.

3 Heat 3 tablespoons of the reserved olive oil in a medium non-stick skillet over medium-high heat for 1 minute. Add the egg mixture, rotating the skillet in a circular motion to distribute it evenly. Lower the heat to medium low and shake the pan a few times to prevent sticking (by shaking the pan, you ensure that the eggs and potatoes release from the pan bottom). Cook the tortilla for about 5 minutes, or until the potatoes on the bottom start to turn golden brown. Place a large flat plate on top of the skillet and invert the skillet. The tortilla should come right out. Add a tablespoon of the reserved olive oil to the skillet and slide the tortilla back in to cook the other side until it is golden brown, about 5 minutes.

4 Turn the heat off and set the skillet aside until the tortilla cools to room temperature. Transfer the tortilla to a plate, sprinkle with parsley, and serve at room temperature cut into triangles or squares.

ham and cheese croquetas

MAKES 8 CROQUETAS

2 tablespoons unsalted butter

¼ cup all-purpose flour

1 cup milk

4 ounces ham, finely chopped

1 cup shredded Gruyère or pepper Jack cheese

¼ teaspoon grated nutmeg

1¼ cups dry bread crumbs

1 large egg

1 cup canola or vegetable oil, for frying

Fig jam, for dipping

chica tip: The combination of the fig jam with the cheese is pure heaven, but if you can't find fig jam, you can serve the croquetas with cubes of guava paste for a similar out-of-this-world flavor combo.

Croquetas remind me of the *cafecitos* ("little coffee shops") in Miami's Little Havana, where these addictive croquetas are served with a cortadito espresso topped with foam. Croquetas are usually made with just ham, but I like to add the richness of cheese to mine. The croqueta batter needs to rest in your fridge for at least four hours before you form and fry the croquetas, so plan accordingly.

1 Melt the butter in a medium skillet over medium-high heat. Take the skillet off the heat and stir in the flour to make a paste. Place the skillet back over medium-high heat and gradually add the milk, whisking constantly, until the mixture is smooth. Let the mixture cook until it is very thick, 3 to 5 minutes.

2 Stir in the ham, cheese, and nutmeg and cook until the mixture pulls away from the sides and bottom of the pan, 5 to 7 minutes. Transfer it to a bowl and cool to room temperature, then cover with plastic wrap and refrigerate for at least 4 hours or overnight.

3 When you are ready to serve, preheat your oven to 250°F.

4 Place the bread crumbs in a shallow dish. Whisk the egg with 1 tablespoon of water in a medium bowl. Roll a walnut-size piece of dough into a 2-inch-long finger-thick croqueta. Repeat with the rest of the dough. Roll each croqueta in the bread crumbs, and then dip it into the egg mixture, turning it to coat. Roll it in the bread crumbs a second time, coating it evenly. Place the breaded croquetas on a baking sheet or platter.

5 Heat the oil in a large skillet until it's very hot and smoking. Add a few croquetas (don't overcrowd the pan or your oil will cool down too much and the croquetas will be oily and heavy) and fry them, turning them in the oil often, until they're brown on all sides, 5 to 7 minutes. Transfer the cooked croquetas to a paper-towel-lined plate and keep warm in the oven while you fry the remaining croquetas. Serve hot with fig jam on the side for dipping.

tomato-mango bruschetta

SERVES 8 TO 10

2 yellow tomatoes, cored, halved, and diced

1 red tomato, cored, halved, and diced

1 mango, peeled, fruit cut off of the seed and diced (see Chica tip)

1 small red onion, finely diced

1½ teaspoons balsamic vinegar

1 tablespoon extra-virgin olive oil, plus more for drizzling

½ cup fresh cilantro or basil leaves

Coarse salt and freshly ground pepper

1 baguette, thinly sliced on a diagonal, or 1 loaf Cuban bread, thinly sliced

3 garlic cloves, halved

These are some of my favorite colors and flavors. I always get compliments on these bruschetta, too, making this a win-win recipe. They're gorgeous on a brunch buffet or a platter of nibbles. If you have a grill, try charring the bread instead of toasting it in the oven for a yummy contrast. I always say that we eat with our eyes, and the yellow tomatoes add tons of visual appeal to the topping. If you can't find any, just use three red tomatoes instead. Stretch the bruschetta topping to serve more people by cutting the baguette into rounds rather than diagonal slices; each slice will have less surface to cover.

1 Preheat your oven to 400°F. Place the tomatoes, mango, onion, balsamic vinegar, oil, cilantro (or basil), and some salt and pepper in a medium bowl. Toss to combine and set aside.

2 Arrange the bread slices on a baking sheet and toast in the oven for 8 to 10 minutes, turning the slices halfway through, until both sides of the bread are lightly browned. Rub the garlic halves vigorously over each slice of bread. Spoon about 1 heaping tablespoon of the tomato and mango mixture onto each bread slice and arrange the bruschetta on a platter. Drizzle with some good-quality olive oil and serve immediately.

chica tip: To cut a mango easily, slice ½ inch off the top and bottom. Stand the mango upright and use a vegetable peeler to remove the skin. Slice off the two wide sides first to get two wide pieces, then slice, cube, or dice. Slice off the two narrow strips next and slice, cube, or dice. Note that the fruit becomes more fibrous the closer it is to the seed.

bacon guacamole

SERVES 6

8 to 10 bacon slices (about ½ pound)

3 medium Hass avocados, halved, seeded, and peeled

1 tomato, halved, cored, seeded, and chopped

1 small red onion, finely chopped

2 serrano chiles, finely chopped (seeded and ribbed for less heat)

3 tablespoons chopped fresh cilantro leaves

3 tablespoons fresh lime juice (from about 1½ limes)

Salt

Guacamole makes me happy because it's always made to be shared with friends. Bacon lends new life to this old-time favorite, but feel free to omit it for an equally addictive classic guacamole. Serve with a mix of black corn and white corn tortilla chips for the prettiest presentation.

1 Heat a large skillet over medium-high heat. Add the bacon and cook until each side is brown and crisp, 7 to 10 minutes total. Transfer the bacon to a paper-towel-lined plate and let it cool completely. Chop the bacon into small bits and set aside.

2 Mash the avocados in a medium bowl until the texture is semi-smooth. Stir in the crumbled bacon. Pat the chopped tomato dry with a paper towel and add to the avocado mixture. Gently stir in the onion, chiles, cilantro, and lime juice. Taste and add salt if necessary; the bacon might add enough saltiness on its own.

chica tip: If you want chopped or sliced tomatoes to contribute their texture and flavor but not their juices to guacamole, an omelet, or a sandwich, blot them with paper towels before using.

guava shells with herbed cheese

SERVES 6

1 15-ounce can guava shells, drained and patted dry

6 ounces goat cheese, farmer cheese, or cream cheese, at room temperature

1 teaspoon garlic salt or 1 tablespoon finely minced shallot

1 tablespoon dried oregano

1 tablespoon dried basil

2 tablespoons chopped fresh chives or scallions

These are so gorgeous that no one ever guesses they take mere minutes to make, and I don't tell them, either! Guava with farmer cheese is a classic South American combination that I play with here. I find fresh garlic overwhelming in this filling, so I use garlic salt instead. If you don't like garlic salt, you can make the filling with some chopped shallot instead. Guava shells are available in cans and are semisoft, tender, and sweet, a little smaller than a peach half. Stunning and elegant, the sweet guava and tangy cheese make quite a pair!

1 Arrange the guava shells on a serving platter. Place the cheese in a bowl and stir in the garlic salt, oregano, and basil.

2 Using a small ice cream scoop or spoon, place a rounded ball of the cheese mixture in each guava shell and sprinkle with some fresh chives. Serve at room temperature on a deviled egg or escargot platter if you have one (the little indentations are perfect holders for the guava cup).

chica tip: Turn a resealable plastic bag into a piping bag for fancy presentations. Place a smooth, soft mixture (such as the herbed cheese or frosting or pâté) in a quart-size resealable plastic bag. Using scissors, cut a small upside-down V into one corner of the bag and squeeze out the filling.

'shroom ceviche

SERVES 6

¾ small red or white onion, finely minced

Salt

18 brown or white button mushroom caps, cleaned and finely chopped

¾ cup fresh cilantro leaves, plus extra for garnish

1 jalapeño pepper (seeded and ribbed for less heat), diced (optional)

⅔ cup fresh lemon juice (from about 2½ lemons), plus 1 lemon cut into wedges for garnish

Freshly ground pepper

Though there are few ingredients in this fresh, healthy, and light ceviche, its flavor is surprisingly beautiful and bold. Serve it in small dishes or glasses; it makes a great quick veggie side dish, too.

1 Sprinkle the minced onion with a few pinches of salt and set aside for 10 minutes (this will reduce the bite of the onion).

2 Combine the mushrooms, onion, cilantro, jalapeño (if using), and lemon juice in a medium bowl. Add salt and pepper to taste, cover with plastic wrap, and refrigerate for at least 30 minutes or overnight (return to room temperature before serving). Sprinkle the ceviche with a few cilantro leaves and serve with lemon wedges.

stuffed mushrooms

SERVES 8

1 8-ounce package cream cheese, softened

¼ pound ham (preferably Serrano), finely chopped

1 teaspoon chopped fresh thyme leaves

Salt

1¼ pounds (2 10-ounce boxes) white "stuffer" mushrooms, cleaned and stems removed

½ pound seedless green grapes

2 tablespoons unsalted butter, melted

¼ cup grated Parmesan cheese

I never loved stuffed mushrooms because they usually contain a bland, bready filling that is too heavy. Not these! The combination of Serrano ham and Parmesan cheese in these stuffed mushrooms is really amazing. They're tender and juicy-sweet from the grapes and a little crispy and salty on top from the cheese.

1 In a small bowl, combine the cream cheese with the ham, thyme, and salt until well blended.

2 Arrange the mushroom caps gills up on a rimmed baking sheet. Place a grape in each cap.

3 Top the grape with a spoonful of the cream cheese mixture. Drizzle some of the melted butter over each mushroom and sprinkle with the grated Parmesan cheese. Cover with plastic wrap and refrigerate for at least 30 minutes or overnight to firm up the filling.

4 Preheat your oven to 400°F.

5 Bake the stuffed mushroom caps until the cheese is browned, 8 to 10 minutes, and serve hot.

arepa chips

SERVES 6 TO 8

1 cup masa arepa or masa harina P.A.N. (see "The Delicioso Pantry," page 10)

1 cup warm water

1 teaspoon olive oil

Coarse salt

Once you try arepa chips, you'll never go back to potato chips. In Latin America (with the exception of Mexico), arepas are the daily bread of choice. Each country and region has its own version, and the flavor and texture vary depending on what kind of flour they're made with, how thick they're rolled, and how large they are. Of course there is much debate over whose are the best! My favorite arepas are the thin and crispy ones from Bogotá; they're positively addictive. I always make a big batch with the intention of eating just a few and freezing the rest in plastic bags, but I usually end up devouring them all! Store uneaten chips in an airtight container with a slice of bread. This will give them a bit of moisture so they don't become too brittle.

1 Preheat your oven to 400°F. Line a baking sheet with parchment paper.

2 Combine the masa arepa with the warm water and olive oil in a medium bowl and mix until the dough comes together into a ball. Divide the ball into 3 equal pieces and roll each out between 2 sheets of plastic wrap to a thickness of ⅛ inch or slightly thinner. Use a 1½-inch cookie cutter to cut the dough into small rounds, then use a small spatula to transfer the rounds onto the baking sheet. Sprinkle the arepas with a pinch of salt.

3 Bake the arepa chips for about 20 minutes, or until they are just starting to turn tan in color. Let the arepa chips cool on the baking sheet, then serve, or store in an airtight container for up to 2 days.

FOR LARGE AREPA CHIPS When cut into large circles, these make a wonderful base for toppings like crab salad (see page 57). Use a 4-inch cookie cutter to cut the arepa dough into about 16 discs. Bake the arepas until crisp and browned and set aside until cooled completely.

crab arepas

SERVES 8

1½ cups lump crabmeat, drained and picked over for shells and cartilage

¾ cup sour cream

6 scallions, light green and white parts only, finely chopped

1 small red onion, finely minced

2 tablespoons minced ají amarillo chile (or 2 tablespoons minced roasted red or yellow peppers plus ½ teaspoon cayenne pepper)

½ teaspoon cayenne pepper

½ teaspoon freshly ground black pepper

Salt

16 toasted Arepa Chips (page 56)

Salmon roe or other red caviar, for garnish (optional)

Made with larger arepa chips, crab arepas are party snacks at their finest. Use any kind of sweet shellfish here, such as precooked shrimp or even lobster if you really feel like showing off. A few grains of salmon roe for garnish gild the lily even further! For sources for ají amarillo, see "The Delicioso Pantry," page 10. A French baguette, sliced and toasted; crostini; or even an endive spear are all excellent stand-ins for the arepas.

1 Place the crabmeat in a medium bowl. Add the sour cream, most of the scallions (save some for garnish), the red onion, ají amarillo (or roasted peppers), cayenne pepper, and black pepper and mix gently until just combined. Season to taste with salt, cover with plastic wrap, and refrigerate until chilled, about 30 minutes or up to 4 hours ahead of time.

2 Top each toasted arepa round with a spoonful of the crab mixture. Garnish with the reserved chopped scallions and a few pearls of salmon roe and serve.

chica tip: Stock up on frozen arepa dough. You can defrost it in your fridge overnight and cut fun shapes from the dough with cookie cutters. Use it instead of toasted bread for bruschetta.

chorizo empanadas

MAKES 20 EMPANADAS

2 large eggs

12 ounces raw chorizo sausages, casings removed

1 yellow onion, chopped

1 cup golden raisins

1 large egg white

Pinch of salt

20 defrosted empanada dough discs (from about 2 10-ounce packages)

Ají sauce (page 102), for serving

chica tip: These are really cute when they're made bite-size. Just cut out the circle shapes using a small cookie cutter and use less filling in each one. Reduce the baking time by 5 to 10 minutes.

The empanada is Latin America's answer to the hamburger. According to legend, empanadas originated in the Middle East and were introduced to the New World by the Spaniards. I like to use natural chorizo if I can find it, since it doesn't have any additives, dyes, or preservatives. It tends to be less salty than traditional chorizo, too. Empanada dough can be found at Latin markets; you can use three defrosted puff pastry sheets instead (they come two to a box), but it will change the texture of the empanada.

1 Preheat your oven to 350°F. Line 2 baking sheets with parchment paper and set aside.

2 Place the whole eggs in a medium saucepan with enough water to cover. Bring the water to a boil, cover the pan, and turn off the heat. Let the eggs sit for 10 minutes, then drain and set aside to cool completely. When they are cool, peel and chop the eggs. Set aside.

3 Heat a medium skillet over medium-high heat for 1 minute. Add the chorizo and the onion (you don't need any additional oil; the chorizo releases enough to fry the onion) and cook until the onion is softened, about 2 minutes. Add the raisins, reduce the heat to medium, and cook until the chorizo is cooked through, about 5 minutes. (Break the chorizo into small bits with a wooden spoon as it cooks.)

4 Whisk the egg white with ½ teaspoon of water and the salt in a small bowl and set aside. Brush the edges of the dough discs with a little egg wash. Place a spoonful of the chorizo filling and a few pieces of the hard-boiled egg on each dough circle. Fold the other end of the dough over and firmly press the edges together, then crimp to seal. Arrange the empanadas on the baking sheet and brush with the egg wash. Bake until golden brown, 25 to 30 minutes. Serve warm or at room temperature with the ají salsa.

salads
and sandwiches

no matter how busy I am, I always stop midday to eat. Lunch is brain food; there's no way I can skip this meal (and with so many tasty dishes to try, why would I want to?). Since I have the rest of the day to burn off the calories, I eat heartily.

When I was a schoolgirl, I used to spend my mornings not concentrating on history or math but daydreaming about lunch. In many Latin homes, lunch is the main meal, and ours was no different. Everyone gathered as a family to eat arroz con pollo or fish croquetas. To this day, my mom still teases me that when she picked me up from school at noon, instead of saying *"¡Hola, Mami!"* I would say "What's for lunch?"

Things haven't changed all that much. When I'm filming, my day often starts at five a.m.; by ten o'clock I am ravenous, and the only thing that gets me through the rest of the morning is thinking about lunch! These days, though, lunch is more likely to be a beautiful salad or an overstuffed sandwich than the hearty feasts my mother dished up. Since I rarely have the luxury of going home for lunch, I focus on the things that travel well and can be eaten on the fly.

Pack a Cheesy Chicken and Pesto Sandwich (page 86) as a brown-bag lunch or Papaya and Feta Salad (page 71) for a picnic, or seal some Golden Sunshine Quinoa Salad (page 74) in a plastic container and take it along to the airport for a healthy food option on the plane. If you do want to make lunch an event like it was at my house, you can't go wrong with "Chicharrones" Fish Tacos with Chipotle Tartar Sauce (page 82), Churrasco Steak Salad (page 79), or one of my favorite recipes, Delicioso Shrimp and Lychee–Stuffed Avocados (page 76).

chiquitita beet salad

SERVES 4

12 whole baby beets or
6 large beets, tops removed
and ends trimmed

2 navel oranges

¼ small Spanish onion,
halved lengthwise and
thinly sliced

¼ cup sliced black olives

10 fresh mint leaves,
coarsely chopped

Salt and freshly ground
pepper

Extra-virgin olive oil

1 tablespoon lime juice
(from about ½ lime)

chica tip: Want to know a carioca's secret for getting a coppery Rio-style tan? Eat lots of beets and drink a glass of beet-and-carrot juice every day for two weeks before leaving for a beach trip!

Ay chiquita—you with the vibrant color and juicy-sweet-tangy-salty flavors and textures! This is one of my favorite salads because it's delicious and so healthy. In fact, even if you don't have time to roast the beets yourself, you should still try this salad with a 14-ounce can of drained, sliced beets. If you do go the extra mile and make the beets from scratch, pick up a pair of rubber or latex gloves from the drugstore to shield your hands and fingernails from beet stains.

1 Preheat your oven to 400°F.

2 If using baby beets, wrap 3 or 4 beets together in foil packets and place them on a baking sheet; if using large beets, wrap them individually in foil and then place on a baking sheet. Roast the beets until they're tender and a paring knife slips easily into their centers, about 20 minutes for baby beets and 45 minutes for large beets. Remove the beets from the oven and, once they are cool enough to handle, open the foil packages. Let the beets cool completely.

3 Meanwhile, peel and segment the oranges. Cut off the tops and bottoms of the oranges so that they sit on the countertop. Using a sharp paring knife, slice off the skin from top to bottom, removing the peel and pith so that no white is left on the orange. Slice along each membrane to cut out the individual orange segments. Place the oranges in a large bowl with the onion, olives, and mint.

4 Slip the beets out of their skins and cut them into ¼-inch-thick slices (halve and then slice if using larger beets). Add them to the bowl with the oranges, season with salt and pepper to taste, and then drizzle some olive oil and the lime juice over the beets. Toss and serve immediately.

arugula, avocado, and fennel salad

SERVES 4 TO 6

2 medium Hass avocados

2 tablespoons fresh lemon juice (from about ½ lemon)

1 fennel bulb, fronds and outer layer removed, cored and very thinly sliced

½ small red onion, thinly sliced

8 cups arugula, washed, dried, and any long or tough stems removed

½ cup fresh cilantro leaves

¼ cup extra-virgin olive oil

Coarse salt and freshly ground pepper

I'm an all-or-nothing kind of girl. For many years, fennel was not my friend; then one day, I woke up and loved it, and I've been on a fennel kick ever since. It's great sliced paper-thin in this salad, but if you don't have a mandoline, just slice it as thin as you can with a sharp knife. Add a tablespoon of orange juice to the dressing and a handful of some toasted pine nuts for an earthy richness. Sprinkle the sliced avocados and fennel with a little lime or lemon juice to prevent them from turning brown.

1 Halve, pit, peel, and slice the avocados and place the slices in a small bowl. Sprinkle with 1 tablespoon of the lemon juice and toss gently to coat. Add the fennel, onion, and the remaining tablespoon of lemon juice and gently toss together.

2 Place the arugula leaves, cilantro, olive oil, and salt and pepper in a large bowl. Add the avocado and fennel mixture and toss together. Serve immediately.

hearts of palm salad

SERVES 6 TO 8

1 ear of corn, husked

4 medium tomatoes, cored, halved, and thinly sliced

2 cups chopped fresh flat-leaf parsley leaves

1 14-ounce can hearts of palm, rinsed, drained, and sliced into ½-inch rounds

Extra-virgin olive oil

Salt and freshly ground pepper

6 leaves of radicchio, for serving

Lime wedges, for serving

This is a real quickie. If you need truly instant gratification, forget charring the corn and slicing it off the cob and just use ⅔ cup of thawed frozen corn instead.

1 Preheat your broiler to high. Place the corn on a baking sheet and roast under the broiler, turning every couple of minutes, until all sides are browned and even a little charred, 6 to 8 minutes. Let the corn cool and then hold it by one end and slice down the cob with a knife to separate the kernels from the cob.

2 Place the corn, tomatoes, parsley, and hearts of palm in a large bowl. Drizzle with some olive oil, season with salt and pepper, and toss together. Scoop the salad into the radicchio cups and serve with lime wedges.

mango, jicama, and radish salad with peanut dressing

SERVES 4 TO 6

3 tablespoons smooth peanut butter

¼ cup fresh lime juice (from about 2 limes)

2 tablespoons light brown sugar

2 tablespoons canola or vegetable oil

Salt

8 large radishes, halved lengthwise and thinly sliced crosswise

6 cups mixed baby greens, washed and dried

1 large or 2 small mangos, peeled, fruit cut off of the seed and cubed (see page 50)

2 cups peeled and cubed jicama (cut into ½-inch cubes)

¼ cup fresh cilantro leaves

Jicama is sweet and crisp, like a cross between an apple and a water chestnut. It grows underground and is native to Mexico. Best of all, jicama doesn't discolor when cut, so it's fantastic in salads. If you can't find it in your market, substitute a green apple, peeled and cut into thin strips, and sprinkle it with some lime juice so it doesn't brown. Sweet, crunchy, and peanutty, this is a kid-friendly salad.

1 Whisk the peanut butter and lime juice in a medium bowl until smooth. Add the brown sugar, oil, and some salt and whisk until combined. Add enough water to thin the sauce and give it a dressing-like consistency, 2 to 3 tablespoons.

2 Place the radishes, greens, mangos, jicama, and cilantro in a large bowl and toss together. Drizzle with the dressing, toss to coat, and serve.

spinach, strawberry, and chayote salad with hello kitty dressing

SERVES 4

3 tablespoons sweetened condensed milk

3 to 4 tablespoons white vinegar

Salt and freshly ground pepper

10 ounces baby spinach

12 strawberries, washed, hulled, and sliced lengthwise

1 chayote squash, peeled, halved, seeded, and sliced into thin strips

This salad reminds me of Hello Kitty: it's sweet, playful, and really girly. Though sweetened condensed milk as a salad dressing base might sound a little funky, it's really good. If you can't find chayote squash, you can use zucchini or yellow summer squash instead. Be sure to wash your spinach really well, even if you use the prewashed bagged kind. Place the greens in a large bowl and cover them with cold water. Swish the leaves around, then pick them up from the bowl and set them aside. Pour out the dirty water, add the spinach back to the bowl, and repeat as many times as necessary until the water in the bowl is clear and free from any little dirt particles after swishing.

1 Whisk the condensed milk, the vinegar (depending on your taste you might need a little extra vinegar), and some salt and pepper together in a small bowl.

2 Place the spinach in a large bowl. Add the strawberries, chayote, and the dressing and toss to coat. Serve immediately.

papaya and feta salad

SERVES 4

6 cups peeled, seeded, and diced papaya (from about 1 large papaya)

½ cup chopped fresh mint leaves

3 tablespoons extra-virgin olive oil

2 tablespoons lime juice (from about 1 lime)

1 tablespoon honey

Salt and freshly ground pepper

1 cup crumbled feta cheese

½ red onion, thinly sliced

I like adding a little of the exotic to my everyday life, and this salad fits the bill beautifully! As odd as fruit with salty cheese might sound, trust me when I say that this salad is amazingly refreshing and tasty. Try it with grilled fish, preferably at a table with a salty breeze and an ocean view on a hot summer day.

1 Place the papaya and mint leaves in a medium bowl. Whisk the olive oil, lime juice, honey, and some salt (add a little salt at first—feta is very salty—you can always add more salt later) and pepper together in a small bowl. Drizzle the dressing over the papaya and toss to coat.

2 Divide the salad among 4 plates; sprinkle with the feta, red onion, and more pepper; and serve.

creamy latin pasta salad

SERVES 6 TO 8

12 ounces rotini pasta
(three quarters of a
16-ounce box)

½ cup evaporated milk

¼ cup extra-virgin olive oil

1 cup crumbled feta cheese

½ cup fresh cilantro leaves

2 tablespoons lime juice
(from about 1 lime)

Salt and freshly ground
pepper

1 cup finely diced ham

1 orange bell pepper, cored,
seeded, ribbed, and
chopped

1 red bell pepper, cored,
seeded, ribbed, and
chopped

¾ cup frozen peas, thawed

½ small red onion, finely
chopped

½ cup chopped and peeled
jicama or celery

½ cup pimento-stuffed
olives

Every *chica* has a secret to making certain dishes. When it comes to my creamy, luscious pasta salad, my until-now secret is really easy: evaporated milk! Make this salad for yourself, and you'll see that it confidently stands up to all of your expectations. The feta cheese adds a nice salty tang, so take a few bites before adding any extra salt—you might not need it.

1 Bring a large pot of salted water to a boil. Add the pasta and cook just past al dente, 14 to 15 minutes. Drain, place in a large bowl, and set aside.

2 While the pasta cooks, combine the evaporated milk, olive oil, feta, cilantro, lime juice, and some salt and pepper in a blender and purée until smooth and creamy. Set aside.

3 Add the ham, bell peppers, peas, onion, jicama (or celery), and olives to the drained pasta. Pour the dressing over the pasta and gently mix it into the salad. Cover with plastic wrap and refrigerate for at least 30 minutes or up to 2 hours before serving.

red bean bikini salad

SERVES 4 TO 6

2 cups dried red kidney beans, soaked in water overnight, or 2 15-ounce cans red kidney beans, rinsed and drained

2 celery stalks, thinly sliced

1 large ripe tomato, cored, halved, and chopped

½ cup chopped sweet pickles

½ small red or yellow onion, thinly sliced

½ cup extra-virgin olive oil

¼ cup cider vinegar

1 teaspoon finely chopped fresh oregano leaves

1 teaspoon Worcestershire sauce

1 teaspoon sugar

½ teaspoon ground cloves

½ teaspoon sweet paprika

Salt and freshly ground pepper

My mom always made this salad for our trips to the beach. We'd take a boat, have a barbecue, and bask under the sun in our bikinis. Actually, I can't remember ever eating this salad without the beach as a backdrop. Mami made it with dried beans soaked in water overnight, but I cheat and use canned beans.

1 If using dried beans, drain the beans and place them in a large pot. Cover with fresh water and bring to a boil. Reduce the heat to medium-low and simmer until the beans are tender, 1 to 1½ hours. If using canned beans, rinse and drain under cold water.

2 Mix the beans, celery, tomato, pickles, and onion together in a large bowl. Whisk the olive oil, vinegar, oregano, Worcestershire sauce, sugar, cloves, paprika, and some salt and pepper together in small bowl. Pour the salad dressing over the beans and toss to coat. Cover with plastic wrap and refrigerate for at least 1 hour or overnight before serving.

golden sunshine quinoa salad

SERVES 6 TO 8

2 cups quinoa

2½ cups homemade or canned low-sodium chicken broth

4 scallions, light and white green parts only, thinly sliced

½ cup golden raisins

3 tablespoons rice vinegar

1 teaspoon grated orange zest

½ cup fresh orange juice (from 2 large oranges)

2 tablespoons extra-virgin olive oil

¼ teaspoon ground cumin

1 cucumber, peeled, halved, seeded, and chopped

½ cup chopped fresh flat-leaf parsley leaves

Salt and freshly ground pepper

A few years ago I went to Bolivia to celebrate my aunt Titi's hundredth birthday. Aunt Titi is my grandfather's sister, and the last living relative of mine from that generation. Her secret to longevity is eating lots of quinoa. I stayed with my family, the Quintanillas, who took me to Lake Titicaca, believed by scientists to be the spot where quinoa was first domesticated by the Incas, and where it is still a major crop. You can almost taste the energy of that land in quinoa.

1 Place the quinoa in a fine-mesh sieve and rinse under cold water until the water runs clear. Bring the chicken broth to a boil in a medium saucepan over medium-high heat. Add the quinoa and return to a boil. Reduce the heat to low, cover, and simmer the quinoa until it has expanded fully, 20 to 25 minutes. Uncover, fluff with a fork, and set aside to cool.

2 Place the cooled quinoa in a large bowl. Add the scallions, raisins, rice vinegar, orange zest and juice, olive oil, cumin, cucumber, and parsley and toss to combine. Season with salt and pepper to taste, cover with plastic wrap, and refrigerate until cold, then serve.

delicioso shrimp and lychee–stuffed avocados

SERVES 4

3 medium Hass avocados

2 lemons, halved

½ cup mayonnaise

1 tablespoon curry powder

Salt

1 pound cooked and peeled small shrimp (60 to 80 per pound)

1 20-ounce can lychee fruit packed in syrup, drained and chopped (about 1 cup)

1 8-ounce can water chestnuts, rinsed, drained, and chopped

2 scallions, light green and white parts only, finely chopped

Chopped fresh cilantro leaves, for garnish

I am a rebel in the kitchen and like to mix up flavors and ingredients from my Latin and American backgrounds. This is one of my favorite salads—not just because it tastes so delicious, but because it really reflects my "a little bit of this and a little bit of that" cooking style. Though lychees originated in China, they now grow in many Latin American countries and are making their way into Latin kitchens. Save the leftover lychee syrup and add it to iced tea or a martini. You can also use it to moisten cake layers or flavor whipped cream.

1 Cut the avocados in half lengthwise and remove the seeds. Carefully peel off the skin while maintaining the avocado's shape. Slice off a sliver from the rounded side of each half so the avocado is stable. Squeeze the lemons all over the avocado halves to keep them from turning brown and set aside.

2 In a large bowl, stir together the mayonnaise and curry powder; season with salt to taste. Gently stir in the shrimp, lychees, water chestnuts, and scallions. Fill the avocado halves with the shrimp mixture and refrigerate for at least 1 hour. Sprinkle with cilantro and serve.

latin caesar with shrimp

SERVES 6 TO 8

½ cup low-fat or regular mayonnaise

2 garlic cloves, finely minced

2 tablespoons red wine vinegar

2 teaspoons Dijon mustard

2 teaspoons Worcestershire sauce

1 teaspoon anchovy paste

¼ teaspoon seeded and chopped canned ají amarillo, or more to taste (optional)

¼ cup chopped fresh cilantro leaves

1 tablespoon olive oil

1½ pounds medium shrimp (40 to 50 per pound), peeled and deveined

Salt and freshly ground pepper

12 cups torn romaine lettuce (from about 1 large head)

2 cups plantain chips

⅓ cup sliced black olives

⅓ cup grated Parmesan cheese

The plantain chips make this salad. If your local store doesn't have them, substitute your favorite croutons instead. The salad can be made with or without the sautéed shrimp, or add grilled or broiled chicken. Ají amarillo is a yellow Peruvian pepper that you can find in Latin markets, or see "The Delicioso Pantry," page 10. Just a little bit of the chile gives the salad dressing a nice edge, but if you don't have any in your pantry, the salad will still taste great.

1 Place the mayonnaise and 1 clove of garlic in a food processor or a blender and process until smooth. While the processor is still running, add the vinegar, mustard, Worcestershire sauce, anchovy paste, ají amarillo (if using), and cilantro and process until blended. Transfer the dressing to a small bowl, cover with plastic wrap, and refrigerate until you're ready to serve.

2 Heat the olive oil in a large skillet over medium-high heat. Add the shrimp and cook, stirring often, until they are almost completely cooked, curled, and opaque, 2 to 3 minutes. Add the remaining clove of garlic and cook, stirring often, until the shrimp are completely opaque and cooked through and the garlic is fragrant, another 1 to 2 minutes. Turn off the heat, sprinkle with some salt and pepper, and set aside to cool slightly so the shrimp don't wilt the greens.

3 Place the lettuce in a large bowl. Add the dressing, toss to coat, and divide the greens among the plates. Sprinkle each serving with some plantain chips, olives, and cheese. Top with the shrimp and serve immediately.

feel-good chicken, chickpea, and artichoke salad

SERVES 4

2 tablespoons olive oil

1 large red onion, chopped

2 garlic cloves, finely minced

2 boneless, skinless chicken breasts halves, finely diced

Salt and freshly ground pepper

3 tablespoons mayonnaise

2 tablespoons fresh lemon juice (from about ½ lemon)

1 tablespoon plus 1½ teaspoons chopped fresh dill, plus extra for garnish

½ teaspoon ground turmeric

1 15-ounce can chickpeas, rinsed and drained

1 14-ounce can artichoke hearts, rinsed, drained, and chopped

4 butterhead lettuce leaves (like Bibb or Boston), washed and dried

Whenever I feel a little stiff and achy, I break out the turmeric. My doctor told me that turmeric is good for my bones, so I got into the habit of adding it to just about everything—stopping just short of adding it to my coffee! This salad brightens up any spread and is sure to get you some "wows," "oohs," and "aahs." Only you will know it's therapeutic, too. This salad is out of this world stuffed into a pita or an arepa for a sandwich.

1 Heat the oil in a large skillet over medium-high heat for 1 minute. Add the onion and garlic and cook, stirring occasionally, until the onion is soft, about 2 minutes. Add the chicken and some salt and pepper and continue to sauté until cooked through, about 3 minutes. Transfer to a plate to cool and set aside.

2 Whisk the mayonnaise, lemon juice, dill, and turmeric together in a large bowl. Add the chickpeas, artichoke hearts, and chicken mixture, stir to combine, and season with salt and pepper to taste. Cover with plastic wrap and refrigerate for 1 hour. Serve the salad in butterhead lettuce cups and garnish with dill.

churrasco steak salad

SERVES 4

½ cup red wine vinegar

3 tablespoons fresh lemon juice (from 1 lemon)

2 teaspoons honey

2 teaspoons coarse salt, plus extra for seasoning the steak

1 tablespoon dried oregano

1 cup extra-virgin olive oil, plus 1 tablespoon olive oil

Freshly ground pepper

1 pound skirt or flank steak

6 cups torn romaine lettuce

4 cups baby arugula

12 cherry tomatoes, halved

½ red onion, thinly sliced

4 ounces Gorgonzola, coarsely crumbled

I am a big steak lover, and flank and skirt steaks are my favorites. They have tons of flavor and little fat, and they don't break the bank. Need I say more? Just sear them in a very hot skillet (these thin steaks are best served pink in the middle) and make sure to let the meat rest before slicing it. This allows the juices to reabsorb into the meat. Reserve any leftover dressing; it makes a great marinade for fish, chicken, and meat.

1 Prepare the vinaigrette by combining the vinegar, lemon juice, honey, 2 teaspoons salt, and the oregano in a medium bowl. Whisk in the cup of olive oil in a thin, steady stream. Season to taste with pepper and set aside.

2 Season the steak with some salt and pepper. Heat the tablespoon of olive oil in a medium skillet or grill pan over medium-high heat for 1 minute. Add the steak and brown for 3 to 4 minutes on each side if you like your steaks done medium-rare or longer for well done. Transfer the steak to a cutting board to rest while you make the salad.

3 Combine the lettuce and arugula in a large bowl. Add the tomatoes, onion, and half of the cheese. Toss the salad with enough of the red wine vinaigrette to lightly coat it. Cut the steaks crosswise into thin slices. Arrange the steak slices on top of the salad and drizzle more vinaigrette over the steak. Sprinkle with the remaining cheese and serve.

chica tip: Store vinaigrette-style salad dressing in a child's sippy cup. You can sprinkle as much as you like onto the salad and keep the rest fresh in the fridge. Just remember to cover the holes in the lid when you shake the dressing!

latin elvis

SERVES 4

1 tablespoon vegetable oil

1 large, very ripe black-skinned plantain, peeled and cut on the diagonal into ¼-inch-thick slices

8 slices raisin bread

¼ to ½ cup smooth or chunky peanut butter

I have had a crush on Elvis Presley since I was young, and I was especially intrigued by his obsession with peanut butter and banana sandwiches. If the King were still alive, you can bet I'd make sure he tried my Latin version! I have to confess that I've been known to make myself one of those rich, comforting sandwiches late at night and then take it to bed with me—just me, Elvis, and a tall glass of milk.

1 Heat the oil in a large skillet over medium-high heat. Add the plantain slices and sauté until they're cooked through and golden brown, 2 to 3 minutes per side. Transfer them to a paper-towel-lined plate to drain and set aside.

2 Spread each slice of bread with peanut butter, spreading it as thin or thick as you like. Arrange a layer of plantain slices on 4 of the bread slices and cover with the remaining slices. Grill on a panini press until toasted and browned on both sides. You can also cook the sandwich as you would a grilled cheese sandwich, with a little butter in a nonstick pan; press the sandwich down using a spatula as it cooks. Slice in half and serve with a glass of milk.

cheesy chicken and pesto sandwiches

MAKES 6 SANDWICHES

- ½ cup basil leaves
- 1 cup crumbled feta cheese
- ¼ cup evaporated milk
- ¼ cup plus 2 tablespoons extra-virgin olive oil
- 2 garlic cloves, finely minced
- 1 tablespoon balsamic vinegar
- Salt and freshly ground pepper
- 4 boneless, skinless chicken breasts halves
- 2 baguettes, cut into thirds, or 6 long rolls, split in half
- 1 head of lettuce, shredded (arugula or watercress also works well)
- 1 red bell pepper, cored, seeded, ribbed, and thinly sliced
- 1 orange bell pepper, cored, seeded, ribbed, and thinly sliced
- 2 tomatoes, cored and sliced

This is not your typical Italian pesto—it is my cheesy Latin friend! For those of you who can't grill year-round like we do in Miami, feel free to broil the chicken breasts for 6 minutes on each side or until they're cooked through. If you don't have the energy to make the marinade, marinate the chicken breasts in Italian dressing instead.

1 Place the basil, feta cheese, evaporated milk, and ¼ cup of the olive oil in a blender or a food processor and purée. Transfer the pesto to a bowl, cover with plastic wrap, and refrigerate for up to 3 days.

2 Place the garlic, balsamic vinegar, the remaining 2 tablespoons of olive oil, and some salt and pepper in a gallon-size resealable plastic bag. Rinse the chicken breasts under cold water, pat them dry, and add to the marinade. Refrigerate the chicken for at least 30 minutes or up to 2 days in advance.

3 Heat your grill to medium (you should be able to hold your hand 5 inches above the grill grates for no more than 5 seconds). Grill the chicken breasts for about 7 minutes on each side, or until they are cooked through. Set aside to cool slightly and then slice into strips.

4 Cut the bread lengthwise but not all the way through. Spread the pesto on the inside of the bread and then add 1 layer of chicken strips. Cover with some of the lettuce, bell peppers, and tomatoes (you can drizzle the veggies with any leftover pesto if you like) and wrap the sandwich in wax paper and then colored napkins. Tie together with kitchen twine and serve.

chica tip: For the most delicious potato chips ever, pour a bag of thick-cut kettle chips into a large bowl and toss with a few dashes of Maggi seasoning sauce and some fresh lime juice!

shrimp and mango wrap-me-ups

MAKES 6 WRAPS

⅓ cup sour cream

⅓ cup mayonnaise

1 tablespoon chopped fresh oregano leaves

2 tablespoons chopped fresh chives

1 tablespoon fresh lime juice (from ½ lime)

Salt and freshly ground pepper

1½ pounds peeled and deveined cooked shrimp, coarsely chopped

1 ripe mango, peeled, fruit cut off of the seed and diced (see page 50)

6 9-inch flour tortillas, warmed

1 bunch of watercress, tough stems removed, washed and dried

Wraps are burritos for the twenty-first century. They're lighter and sleeker and are filled with much sexier ingredients, such as mangos and fresh herbs. I got turned on to wraps a few years ago, and now I find myself making and eating them all the time, for quick on-the-go food, for party pass-arounds, or for a late-night fix. Wraps are still one of my favorite food fads. They fit perfectly into my shortcut-loving lifestyle: There's no need for a starch or veggie side dish because everything is already included. They're really tasty with avocados, some cilantro, and whatever sauce you happen to have in the fridge.

1 Pulse the sour cream, mayonnaise, oregano, chives, lime juice, and some salt and pepper in a blender or a food processor until the mixture is pale green. Transfer the mixture to a medium bowl, add the shrimp and mangos, and stir to combine.

2 Heat a small skillet over medium-high heat. Add a tortilla and warm on each side for 10 to 15 seconds, or until it is heated through.

3 Arrange some watercress in the center of each tortilla. Top with some of the shrimp mixture. Fold in the sides and then roll the tortilla tightly to enclose the filling. Cut the wraps on the diagonal and serve.

chica tip: To warm tortillas in the microwave, stack them on a plate and cover with a damp cloth. Microwave for 30 seconds and keep them covered until you're ready to serve them.

for me, soup is soul food. It's easy to make and inexpensive; a pot lasts for days; it's comforting, nutritious, and, most important, really delicious. In Colombia, we often refer to a meal as *jugo sopa y seco,* meaning "juice, soup, and dry." Typically you're served the broth of the soup first, followed by the meat, chicken, plantains, vegetables, and potatoes with rice on the side. It's not fancy or elegant—just real food. Even thinking about soup gives me hunger pangs.

I grew up with lots of *sopitas* (little soups) on the table and they are a big part of my diet. Whether for dinner or packed in a plastic container for lunch, soup is an affordable and easy way to work healthy foods into your diet, too. Often light and always nutritious, they offer lots of brain food in the form of energizing vitamins and minerals. Instead of adding cream or potatoes as a thickener, I often count on the vegetables and starches themselves to break down and make the soup luscious and creamy.

While I love hot soups, like Plantain Soup (page 97) and Sopi Piska (page 100), some of my favorite soups are cool cold ones. Cold soups are pretty common in Latin America because they're so easy to make, refreshing, and fun to serve. I especially like portioning them out in shot glasses for chic starters. Tropical Pineapple Gazpacho (page 91) and Chill-Out Honeydew Soup with Ham (page 92) take no time to make and are light-hearted additions to brunch, cocktails, lunch, or whatever. Whether you use them to warm you from the inside out or to cool you down on a deliciously hot day, these *sopitas* are pure comfort in a bowl.

tropical pineapple gazpacho

SERVES 6

1 large pineapple, cored and peeled

3 medium cucumbers, peeled, halved, and seeded

1 cup pineapple juice

1 jalapeño, halved, seeded, and finely diced

1 scallion, light green and white parts only, thinly sliced

1 tablespoon sea salt

12 ounces green seedless grapes, halved (about 2 cups)

1 teaspoon lime juice, plus lime wedges for serving

2 tablespoons fresh cilantro leaves, plus a few sprigs of cilantro for garnish

3 tablespoons extra-virgin olive oil (optional), plus more for serving

¼ cup finely chopped macadamia nuts

Dios mío, **how many veggie plates and salads can a** *chica* **eat? When I'm too bored with lettuce to even look at it, this is what I make. It's** *fabuloso* **for lunch, especially on a hot, hot day, and is a great, unexpected starter for entertaining.**

1 Cut half of the pineapple and half of the cucumbers into large chunks (reserve the rest) and place in a blender. Add the pineapple juice, jalapeño, scallion, and salt to the blender and purée. Cut the reserved pineapple and cucumber into small (½-inch) cubes and add to the blender with the grapes, lime juice, cilantro, and the olive oil (if using). Pulse 2 to 3 times (you want the pineapples and cucumbers to remain a little chunky).

2 Stir the purée and taste and season with more lime juice or salt if necessary. Cover the bowl with plastic wrap and refrigerate for 1 hour before serving. Divide the gazpacho among 6 bowls. Sprinkle with the chopped macadamia nuts, garnish with a drizzle of olive oil and the cilantro sprigs, and serve with lime wedges on the side.

chill-out honeydew soup with ham

SERVES 4

2 pounds very cold honeydew melon, peeled, halved, seeded, and coarsely chopped (about 5 cups of melon)

¼ cup fresh mint leaves, plus a few extra chopped leaves for garnish

2 tablespoons plus 1½ teaspoons sour cream

1 cup diced Serrano ham

1 lime, cut into wedges, for serving

The salty-sweet-tangy combination in this twist on the classic prosciutto-wrapped melon is amazing. It's so fast to make that I often prepare it for last-minute brunches: Pair it with huevos rancheros and mimosas and you're golden.

1 Chill 4 soup bowls in your refrigerator.

2 Place the melon and mint in a blender and purée. Add the sour cream and continue to process until completely incorporated. Divide the soup among the chilled bowls, sprinkle each with some diced ham and chopped mint, and serve with a lime wedge.

chipotle and black-eyed pea soup

SERVES 4

1 tablespoon olive oil

1 large yellow onion, peeled and coarsely chopped

2 garlic cloves

½ teaspoon dried rosemary

½ teaspoon dried thyme

2 cups frozen black-eyed peas

5 cups homemade or canned low-sodium chicken broth

½ canned chipotle chile en adobo, split and seeded

Salt and freshly ground pepper

Plain yogurt, for garnish

Chopped fresh cilantro leaves, for garnish

Lime wedges, for serving

It's hard to believe that any soup this creamy, smoky, and seductive could be so simple to make. It tastes really sinful even though it's made with just 1 tablespoon of oil. The yogurt's cool tang is a great contrast to the spicy chipotle flavor.

1 Heat the olive oil in a large saucepan over medium-high heat for 1 minute. Add the onion and garlic and cook, stirring occasionally, until the onion is soft, about 2 minutes. Add the dried herbs and cook until they're fragrant, 2 to 3 minutes. Add the frozen black-eyed peas and the chicken broth, bring to a boil for 3 minutes, lower the heat to medium low, and simmer, partially covered, for 40 minutes.

2 Pour a few ladles of the black-eyed pea mixture into a blender and purée. (When blending hot liquids, fill the blender less than halfway full, place the lid askew, and pulse the liquid at first to release some of the heat; otherwise, your blender top could pop!) Transfer the soup to a clean pot and repeat with the remaining black-eyed peas, adding the chipotle chile to the last batch. Bring the soup to a simmer and season with salt and pepper to taste. Top each portion with a dollop of plain yogurt, sprinkle with chopped cilantro, and serve with a lime wedge.

yummy avocado sopita

SERVES 4

1 tablespoon unsalted butter

1 white onion, finely chopped

2 garlic cloves, peeled and smashed

½ red, orange, or yellow bell pepper, cored, seeded, ribbed, and finely chopped

1 tablespoon plus 1½ teaspoons chopped fresh dill

Salt and freshly ground pepper

½ cup heavy cream

3 medium Hass avocados, halved, seeded, peeled, and coarsely chopped

1 cup milk

2 tablespoons olive oil

16 small raw shrimp, peeled and deveined

Fresh basil leaves, finely chopped, for garnish

Sesame seeds, for garnish

In the surfer town of Playa del Coco, Costa Rica, there is a cute little restaurant called El Chile Dulce. After a day of sun and sand, nothing was more welcome than this gorgeous pale green soup. Sipping a luscious and silky spoonful is like slipping into something a little more comfortable. I call this a sopita—"little soup"—because it's so rich you should serve it in small portions.

1 Melt the butter in a medium skillet over medium-high heat. Add the onion, garlic, and bell peppers and cook, stirring occasionally, until the vegetables are soft, 4 to 6 minutes. Add the dill and some salt and pepper to taste. Stir in the cream and pour the mixture into a blender.

2 Add the avocados, milk, and 1 tablespoon of the olive oil to the blender and purée. When the purée is completely smooth, transfer it to a bowl, cover, and refrigerate until chilled (the soup can be made up to 1 day in advance).

3 Heat the remaining tablespoon of olive oil in a medium skillet over medium-high heat. Add the shrimp and cook until curled, pink, and opaque, 2 to 4 minutes. To serve, pour the chilled soup into small glasses, add some of the shrimp, and garnish with basil and sesame seeds.

chica tip: Avocados are wonderful for your hair. Mash some up and comb it through your hair. Wrap the top of your head in plastic wrap and read a book or surf the Web for 20 minutes, then rinse out.

queen of hearts soup

SERVES 4

1 tablespoon unsalted butter

½ medium white onion, finely chopped

2 cups homemade or canned low-sodium chicken broth

1 cup half-and-half

1 14-ounce can hearts of palm, rinsed, drained, and chopped

½ canned chipotle chile en adobo, seeded and finely chopped

1 teaspoon salt, plus more to taste

Freshly ground pepper

2 teaspoons finely chopped fresh flat-leaf parsley

You know how it is when you're hungry and you just have nothing to eat in the fridge? When this happens to me, I turn to my pantry for inspiration. This soup is the result of one of my pantry adventures, and it is totally unique and wonderful. It's the best reason I can think of to make sure that I always have hearts of palm and chipotles on hand!

1 Melt the butter in a large saucepan over medium heat. Add the onion and cook, stirring occasionally, until it is soft and translucent, about 2 minutes. Add the broth, half-and-half, hearts of palm, chipotle en adobo, and salt and bring to a boil. Reduce the heat to medium low, cover partially, and simmer for 5 minutes.

2 Ladle some of the soup into a blender and purée until it's completely smooth. (When blending hot liquids, fill the blender less than halfway full, place the lid askew, and pulse the liquid at first to release some of the heat; otherwise, your blender top could pop!) Transfer the puréed soup to a clean saucepan and repeat with the remaining soup. Bring the soup to a boil over medium-low heat, stirring frequently. Season with salt and pepper to taste, sprinkle with parsley, and serve.

plantain soup

SERVES 6 TO 8

1 tablespoon olive oil

1 small yellow onion, finely chopped

1 carrot, peeled and finely chopped

1 celery stalk, strings removed and finely chopped

2 garlic cloves, finely chopped

4½ cups homemade or canned low-sodium chicken broth, plus extra if needed

2 green plantains, peeled and thinly sliced

1 cup finely chopped fresh cilantro leaves, some reserved for garnish

2 bay leaves

½ teaspoon ground cumin

Salt and freshly ground pepper

If the name of this soup brings to mind a bowl of puréed bananas, you are in for a revelation! While the plantains do have a hint of sweetness, the soup is not at all cloying, and instead has an intriguing sweet-salty flavor that is nothing short of amazing. Rip off a big hunk of bread and taste what you've been missing.

1 Heat the olive oil in a medium saucepan over medium-high heat for 1 minute. Add the onion, carrot, celery, and garlic and cook, stirring often, until the onion is soft and browned, about 8 minutes. Add the chicken broth, plantains, cilantro, bay leaves, and cumin; bring to a boil, reduce the heat to the lowest setting, and cook at a bare simmer, uncovered, until the plantains are very tender, about 45 minutes. Discard the bay leaves.

2 Transfer half of the soup to a blender and purée until smooth. (When blending hot liquids, fill the blender less than halfway full, place the lid askew, and pulse the liquid at first to release some of the heat; otherwise, your blender top could pop!) Stir the puréed soup back into the pot with the remaining chunky soup and mix well. If the soup is too thick for your taste, add more chicken broth. Season to taste with salt and pepper, sprinkle with the reserved cilantro, and serve.

chica tip: To peel a hard green plantain, make a slit in the peel from top to bottom on each side of the plantain, and then just slip off the peel.

south-of-the-border bouillabaisse

SERVES 6 TO 8

2 tablespoons olive oil

2 celery stalks, diced

2 yellow onions, diced

2 red bell peppers, cored, seeded, ribbed, and diced

2 poblano peppers, cored, seeded, ribbed, and diced

2 large tomatoes, peeled, cored, and diced

4 garlic cloves, finely minced

1 cup tomato paste

1 tablespoon chopped fresh oregano leaves

1 teaspoon chopped fresh thyme leaves

Salt and freshly ground pepper

5 cups fish broth or stock

1 14-ounce can coconut milk

1 cup dry white wine

1 8-ounce salmon fillet, cut into 1-inch chunks

1 8-ounce red or yellowtail snapper fillet, cut into 1-inch chunks

1 pound calamari cut into ½-inch rings

8 ounces small scallops

1 pound large shrimp, peeled and deveined

1 pound mussels in their shells, debearded and scrubbed

½ cup finely chopped fresh cilantro leaves

1 baguette, sliced, for serving

There are hints of South America, the Caribbean, and, yes, even France in this fish stew. Many home cooks shy away from making bouillabaisse because the added step of making the fish stock seems intimidating. That's a shame, because bouillabaisse is one of the most elegant and impressive dishes for entertaining. So let's leave the très compliqué to the French chefs—it makes them feel important! I prefer feeling like a clever chica. Buy a good-quality organic fish stock at the market. It tastes wonderful and saves a lot of time. And because coconut milk gives the broth a silky richness, you can skip the traditional rouille, too!

1 Heat the oil in a large pot over medium-high heat. Add the celery, onions, bell and poblano peppers, tomatoes, and garlic and cook, stirring occasionally, until the vegetables are soft, 5 to 7 minutes. Mix in the tomato paste, oregano, thyme, and some salt and pepper and cook, stirring often, for 1 to 2 minutes, or until the herbs are fragrant.

2 Add the fish broth, coconut milk, and wine and bring to a boil. Reduce the heat to low, cover, and simmer for 8 minutes. Add the salmon and snapper, cover, and cook for 3 minutes. Add the calamari, scallops, shrimp, and mussels, cover, and cook until the mussels open and the shrimp and fish are opaque and cooked through, 3 to 5 minutes longer. (Discard any mussels that don't open.) Sprinkle with the cilantro and serve in shallow bowls with the bread.

sopi piska (curaçao fish soup)

SERVES 4 TO 6

1 tablespoon canola oil

4 scallions, white and light green parts only, finely chopped

1 medium yellow onion, chopped

½ green bell pepper, seeds and ribs removed, finely diced

½ red bell pepper, seeds and ribs removed, finely diced

2 large carrots, finely diced

2 celery stalks, finely diced

½ cup diced canned tomatoes

2 tablespoons Maggi seasoning sauce or Worcestershire sauce

1 tablespoon dried oregano

4 cups homemade or canned low-sodium chicken broth

2 tablespoons tomato paste

¼ of a fresh habanero pepper, seeded

1½ pounds skinless red snapper fillets, cut into 1-inch cubes

Salt and freshly ground pepper

Lime wedges, for serving

1 baguette, sliced, for serving

I spent part of my childhood in Curaçao, and every Sunday, my whole family would go to the Curaçao Yacht Club, Jan Christian, or Playa Forti restaurants just to eat sopi piska, a wonderfully chunky fish soup. The fish was hauled in fresh daily, and the soup was served with lots of limes and finished with a Madame Janette hot pepper. I make it whenever I need a taste of home, or whenever I have a hangover: This along with a Michelada María (page 223) is the best day-after remedy! Serve it with fried polenta or sliced French bread.

1 Heat the oil in a large pot over medium-high heat for 1 minute. Add the scallions, onion, bell peppers, carrots, and celery and let them cook over medium heat, stirring often, until they're very soft, about 10 minutes. Add the tomatoes, the Maggi seasoning sauce, and the oregano. Continue to cook until the liquid has nearly evaporated, 5 more minutes.

2 Add the chicken broth, 2 cups of water, the tomato paste, and the habanero pepper and bring to a simmer. Add the fish and let it simmer until it's cooked through, about 15 minutes. Remove and discard the piece of habanero pepper. Season the soup with salt and pepper to taste and serve hot with a lime wedge and baguette slices.

peruvian chicken soup for the soul (aguadito)

SERVES 6

1 tablespoon canola or vegetable oil

6 chicken drumsticks, skin and excess fat removed

3 garlic cloves, finely minced

1½ medium yellow onions, finely chopped

1 large carrot, finely diced

1 cup white rice

¾ cup frozen peas

2½ tablespoons culantro paste (or 2 cups fresh culantro or cilantro puréed in a food processor with 1 teaspoon canola or vegetable oil)

7 cups homemade or canned low-sodium chicken broth

2 teaspoons salt

Sauce from a can of ají amarillo or a habanero hot sauce, for serving (optional)

Lime wedges, for serving

This is mega comfort food, and I have chased away the worries of more than one bad day with a giant bowlful. You can find culantro in Latin markets, either fresh or in paste form. It's a long-leaf herb with a flavor like that of strong cilantro. I like to drizzle a little of the sauce from a can of ají amarillo into the soup to give it a little heat. A dash of Tabasco sauce, a pinch of cayenne pepper, or a teeny bit of adobo sauce from a can of chipotle chiles en adobo does the same trick; see "The Delicioso Pantry," page 10, for information about buying ají amarillo.

1 Heat the oil in a large pot over medium-high heat. Add the drumsticks and fry until the chicken is browned on one side, about 5 minutes. Turn the chicken pieces and cook for 4 minutes. Add one third of the garlic and continue to cook until the chicken is browned, another 1 to 2 minutes. Transfer the chicken to a plate and set aside. Add the onions, carrot, and the remaining garlic to the pot and cook until the onions are soft and translucent, 3 to 5 minutes. Stir in the rice, the frozen peas, and the culantro paste, making sure all of the rice grains are coated with the herbs. Add 6 cups of the chicken broth, then add the salt and the chicken legs.

2 Bring the liquid to a boil and reduce the heat to medium low. Simmer uncovered until the rice grains split open, about 30 minutes. If the rice becomes dry at any time before the grains split open, add some of the remaining cup of broth, or water.

3 Remove the chicken legs from the pot and carefully pull the chicken meat off the bones using a fork. Return the chicken meat to the pot and mix it in with the rice. Add a drizzle of the ají amarillo sauce (if using) and serve in bowls with a lime wedge.

all-in-one soup with
spicy scallion-lime ají sauce

SERVES 6

FOR THE AJÍ SAUCE

1 cup finely chopped fresh cilantro

8 scallions, white and light green parts only, finely chopped

½ small Scotch bonnet or habanero chile, seeded and finely chopped

1 tablespoon finely chopped white onion

2 teaspoons fresh lime juice

1 small plum tomato, cored and finely chopped (optional)

Salt

FOR THE SOUP

3 tablespoons olive oil

2 large yellow onions, finely chopped

3 garlic cloves, finely minced

2 large tomatoes, cored, peeled, seeded, and chopped

3 bay leaves

1 tablespoon finely chopped fresh thyme leaves

2 pounds chicken thighs, trimmed of excess fat, rinsed and patted dry

This is a very filling dish known as sancocho. Traditionally the meat, plantains, and potatoes are served separately from the broth. It's like two courses in one pot. Ají sauce can be used to spice up just about anything from chicken, potatoes, and soups to empanadas or plain rice. It's used like salt and pepper to add a bit of oomph to anything you can think of (but dessert). Serve sancocho to me with some of the spicy scallion ají sauce and plenty of tortillas or arepas for scooping up the yummy meat and broth and I'll be your best friend for life.

1 To make the ají sauce, place the cilantro, scallions, chile, onion, lime juice, and ¾ cup of water in a small glass bowl or jar with a tight-fitting lid. Add the tomato (if using), season with salt to taste, and stir all of the ingredients together. [Set the sauce aside at room temperature for several hours to allow the flavors to release into the liquid, then refrigerate until serving.]

2 To make the soup, heat the oil in a large stockpot over medium heat for 1 minute. Add the onions and garlic and cook, stirring occasionally, until they're soft and transparent, about 5 minutes. Add the tomatoes, bay leaves, and thyme and continue to cook for 5 more minutes. Add the chicken and the beef ribs and cook, stirring occasionally and skimming the foam from the top of the broth when necessary, until the tomatoes have disintegrated, about 15 minutes. Add the plantains, cilantro, and chicken broth and bring to a boil. Reduce the heat to medium low and simmer, covered, until the plantains are tender, about 30 minutes.

2 pounds beef flanken ribs (also called cross-cut ribs)

2 green plantains, peeled and cut into 2-inch-long pieces

2 ripe plantains, peeled and cut into 2-inch-long pieces

1 large bunch of fresh cilantro, stems tied together with kitchen twine

14 cups homemade or canned low-sodium chicken broth

1½ pounds small red or white potatoes, peeled

4 ears of corn, husked and quartered

10 2-inch-long pieces of frozen yucca

White rice, for serving (optional)

2 medium Hass avocados, halved, seeded, peeled, and sliced, for serving (optional)

Arepas or tortillas, for serving (optional)

3 Using a slotted spoon, remove the chicken from the pot and set it aside. Add the potatoes, corn, and yucca and simmer, uncovered, until they are tender, about 20 minutes. Remove the cilantro and the bay leaves and return the chicken to the pot to reheat it.

4 To serve, arrange a piece of chicken, some beef, plantains, and a few chunks of yucca and potatoes on each plate. Serve the broth in a small bowl, with the ají sauce on the side, along with a bowl of rice and some avocados and arepas or tortillas on separate plates.

ciao
pescao!

from Cuba to Mexico to Colombia, most Latin countries have beautiful seacoasts, and their cuisines are influenced by the sea's bounty. Their traditional and *delicioso* fish and seafood dishes include ceviche, seafood soups, grilled fish, and shrimp salads. It's no wonder that some of my happiest memories seem to revolve around the sea.

Fish and shellfish are both so quick and simple to make, either for many or just one or two. Most recipes can be completed from start to finish in 30 minutes or less, making them excellent as last-minute throw-together meals.

I have a few favorites that I eat all the time, such as mild and delicate tilapia, flavorful and juicy snapper, robust salmon, and succulent shrimp. When I shop for shrimp, I usually buy bags of frozen, shell-on shrimp that have already been deveined. A couple of hours before I want to cook it, I submerge the whole bag in a large bowl of cold water in my sink and leave it there. When I come back to it, the shrimp are defrosted enough to peel and cook. Since virtually all the shrimp we buy has been frozen shortly after being harvested, buying frozen shrimp lets you control the amount of time they spend defrosted. Who knows how long the "fresh" shrimp at your supermarket has been sitting on ice since it was defrosted.

Fish should always smell clean, like the ocean, not fishy. The meat should be firm and glistening, not pasty or soft. Try to cook your fish and shellfish the same day that you buy it, or the day after; the quality will definitely begin to deteriorate if you keep it much longer than that. Of course you can substitute any of your own favorites in the recipes that follow: Try flounder or sole for tilapia; sea bass, pompano, or grouper for snapper; arctic char, tuna, or striped bass for salmon; monkfish or tuna for mahimahi; and mussels, lobster, clams, or scallops for shrimp.

easy breezy coconut ceviche

SERVES 6 TO 8

1½ pounds skinless red snapper fillet, diced, or bay scallops

½ cup fresh lime juice (from about 4 limes)

⅓ cup sweetened shredded coconut, plus extra for serving

1½ small red onion, halved and thinly sliced

2 jalapeños, seeds removed, thinly sliced in rounds

1¼ cup raisins

½ cup coconut milk

¼ cup chopped fresh cilantro leaves, plus extra for serving

1 tablespoon chopped fresh oregano leaves

Salt and freshly ground pepper

Tortilla chips, plantain chips, or canchita (see page 111), for serving (optional)

Snapper is a very ceviche-friendly fish. It isn't very expensive, so consider serving ceviche at a dinner party; you'll give your guests a sophisticated, yummy starter and you'll still be able to put some cash away for the shoe fund! (See photo, page 109.)

1 Place the snapper in a medium bowl and toss gently with the lime juice. Cover the bowl with plastic wrap and refrigerate for at least 30 minutes or up to 1 hour.

2 Preheat your oven to 350°F. Place the coconut on a rimmed baking sheet and toast, shaking the baking sheet every few minutes so the coconut toasts evenly, until golden brown, about 10 minutes. Set aside.

3 Drain the fish and transfer it to a clean bowl (discard the marinade). Add the onion, jalapeños, raisins, toasted coconut, coconut milk, cilantro, oregano, and salt and pepper to taste. Mix well. Cover with plastic wrap and refrigerate for at least 30 minutes or up to 3 hours. Sprinkle with the extra cilantro and the reserved toasted coconut and serve with tortilla chips, plantain chips, or canchita on the side.

 chica tip: To avoid bitterness from limes, rinse your hands with water after squeezing each lime. The bitterness can come from the natural oils in the peel that come off on your hands and run into the juice when you squeeze the limes repeatedly.

salmon ceviche with mango

SERVES 6 TO 8

4 6-ounce skinless salmon fillets, cut into small cubes

1 cup fresh orange juice (from about 2 large oranges)

½ cup fresh lemon juice (from about 3 lemons)

½ cup fresh lime juice (from about 4 limes)

½ cup soy sauce

½ cup mirin

1 red onion, halved and thinly sliced

1 mango, peeled, fruit cut off of the seed and diced (see page 50)

2 to 3 jalapeños (depending on how spicy you like your ceviche), sliced into rings, seeds removed

¾ cup fresh cilantro leaves

Tortilla chips, plantain chips, or canchita (see page 111), for serving

Ceviche is a great light dinner or starter that is made without the oven or stovetop; in fact, you stir it together in one dish, let it marinate for an hour, and there you have it, an instant healthy meal. I like to mix flavors from all over the world in my ceviche, and I have been especially influenced by the fish dishes of Southeast Asia and Japan.

1 Place the salmon in a medium bowl and mix with the orange, lemon, and lime juices. Cover with plastic wrap and refrigerate for at least 20 minutes or up to 1 hour. Drain the salmon, discarding the marinade, and pat it dry with paper towels. Place it in a clean bowl, and if not serving immediately, cover with plastic wrap and refrigerate until you're ready to serve or up to 1 hour.

2 Just before serving, stir the soy sauce, mirin, onion, mango, jalapeños, and cilantro into the salmon. Toss to coat and serve immediately with the tortilla chips, plantain chips, or canchita.

From top to bottom:
Easy Breezy Coconut Ceviche;
Salmon Ceviche with Mango;
Minty-Cool Shrimp Cevich

minty-cool shrimp ceviche

SERVES 6 TO 8

1 pound medium shrimp, tails removed, peeled and deveined

½ cup lime juice (from about 4 limes), plus lime wedges for serving

1 small jalapeño, halved, seeded, and finely chopped

1 medium red onion, halved and thinly sliced

2 cups ½-inch seedless watermelon cubes

¼ cup finely chopped fresh mint leaves, plus a few sprigs for garnish

Coarse sea salt and freshly ground pepper

Extra-virgin olive oil, for drizzling

Tortilla chips, plantain chips, or canchita (see page 111), for serving (optional)

Beachy and refreshing Latin and Caribbean flavors come together to make this fresh-tasting cooked-shrimp ceviche. The crunch of coarse sea salt is fabulous paired with the sweet watermelon and spicy jalapeños. This is a good ceviche to serve to those who might be wary of eating raw seafood. (See photo, page 109.)

1 Bring a large pot of salted water to a boil and add the shrimp. Immediately turn off the heat and let the shrimp sit in the hot water until they're just cooked through, 2 to 3 minutes. Drain and place the shrimp in a large bowl. Add the lime juice and the jalapeño, cover with plastic wrap, and refrigerate for at least 10 minutes or up to 1 hour.

2 When you're ready to serve the ceviche, pour off all but 1 tablespoon of the lime juice and add the red onion, watermelon, mint, and salt and pepper to taste. Drizzle with olive oil and serve immediately with a lime wedge, a mint sprig, and some tortilla chips, plantain chips, or canchita on the side.

chica tip: A serrated grapefruit spoon is excellent for seeding and ribbing jalapeños and keeps your fingers far away from the chiles' spicy juices.

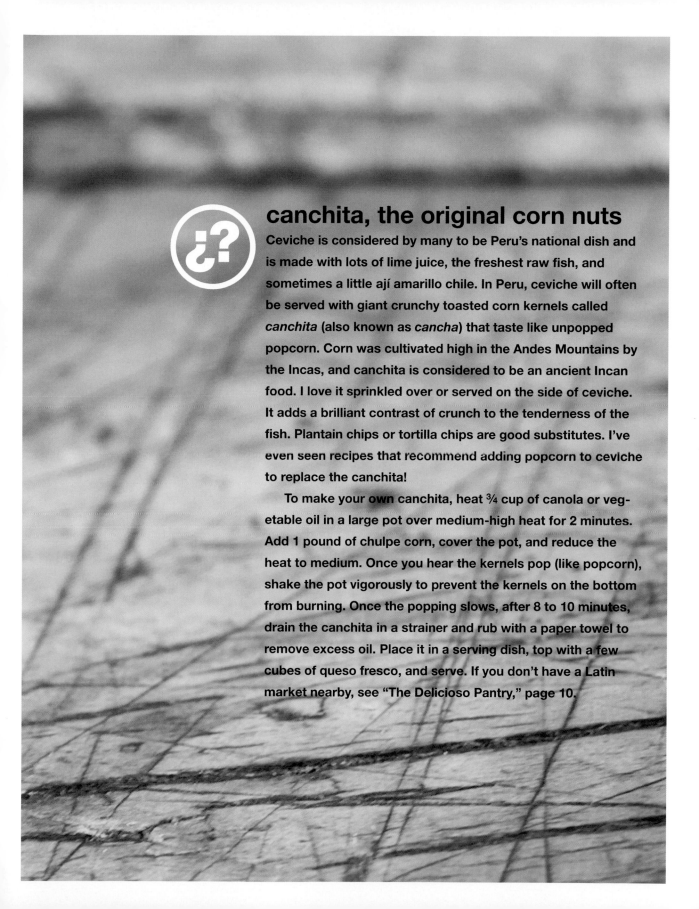

canchita, the original corn nuts

Ceviche is considered by many to be Peru's national dish and is made with lots of lime juice, the freshest raw fish, and sometimes a little ají amarillo chile. In Peru, ceviche will often be served with giant crunchy toasted corn kernels called *canchita* (also known as *cancha*) that taste like unpopped popcorn. Corn was cultivated high in the Andes Mountains by the Incas, and canchita is considered to be an ancient Incan food. I love it sprinkled over or served on the side of ceviche. It adds a brilliant contrast of crunch to the tenderness of the fish. Plantain chips or tortilla chips are good substitutes. I've even seen recipes that recommend adding popcorn to ceviche to replace the canchita!

To make your own canchita, heat ¾ cup of canola or vegetable oil in a large pot over medium-high heat for 2 minutes. Add 1 pound of chulpe corn, cover the pot, and reduce the heat to medium. Once you hear the kernels pop (like popcorn), shake the pot vigorously to prevent the kernels on the bottom from burning. Once the popping slows, after 8 to 10 minutes, drain the canchita in a strainer and rub with a paper towel to remove excess oil. Place it in a serving dish, top with a few cubes of queso fresco, and serve. If you don't have a Latin market nearby, see "The Delicioso Pantry," page 10.

caribbean salmon with mango-veggie salsa and guava barbecue sauce

SERVES 6

FOR THE BARBECUE SAUCE

3 tablespoons vegetable oil

2 yellow onions, chopped

8 ounces guava paste, cut into chunks

3 tablespoons tomato paste

2 tablespoons apple cider vinegar

2 whole star anise

½ teaspoon ground allspice

¼ teaspoon curry powder

3 tablespoons lime juice

1 tablespoon dark rum

FOR THE SALSA

½ cup olive oil, plus extra for greasing the baking dish

3 garlic cloves, finely minced

¼ cup lime juice (from about 2 limes), plus 2 limes cut into wedges for serving

1 teaspoon salt

1 teaspoon freshly ground pepper

2 mangos, peeled, fruit cut off of the seed and diced (see page 50)

This is one of my absolute favorite recipes. In fact, there was a year when my friends would come over for dinner and say, "I bet I know what we're eating for dinner!" If you need to feed a lot of people relatively inexpensively, then this is your dish. Mango-veggie salsa makes a bed for the fish, creating a beautiful presentation as well as a built-in side dish. With some rice on the side, you have everything you need for an excellent "ooh" and "aah" kind of meal. If you don't have time to make the barbecue sauce, stir ½ cup of guava jam or jelly into 1½ cups of your favorite brand of barbecue sauce.

1 To make the barbecue sauce, heat the oil in a large skillet over medium-high heat for 1 minute. Reduce the heat to medium, add the onions, and cook, stirring often, until they're soft and a little brown around the edges, 5 to 7 minutes. Stir in the guava paste, tomato paste, vinegar, star anise, allspice, and curry powder. Simmer, stirring occasionally, until the guava paste has melted, about 15 minutes. Turn off the heat and let the sauce cool slightly. Whisk in the lime juice and rum, transfer to a small bowl, and set aside, or cover with plastic wrap and refrigerate for up to 2 weeks.

2 To make the salsa, whisk the olive oil, garlic, lime juice, salt, and pepper together in a large bowl. Add the mangos, bell peppers, red onion, chile (if using), and cilantro and toss to coat. Add the beans and gently toss everything together.

3 Heat your broiler to high. Line a large baking dish or rimmed baking sheet with a double layer of aluminum foil and grease the foil with some olive oil or nonstick cooking spray.

(recipe continues)

1 red bell pepper, cored, seeded, ribbed, and finely diced

1 green bell pepper, cored, seeded, ribbed, and finely diced

1 yellow bell pepper, cored, seeded and finely diced

1 large red onion, halved and finely chopped

1 serrano chile, finely chopped (optional)

½ cup finely chopped fresh cilantro leaves

1 15-ounce can black beans, rinsed and drained

1 whole side of salmon, 3½ to 4 pounds

4 Place the salmon in the prepared baking dish and tuck about 2 inches of the tail end under the fish, so you have a somewhat uniform shape. Pour the barbecue sauce over the salmon and cook it under the broiler until the sauce caramelizes and chars around the edges and the salmon is firm and flakes easily, 8 to 12 minutes for rare (the salmon will still be pink in the middle) or 12 to 15 minutes for well done (the salmon will be cooked throughout).

5 Spread the salsa on a serving platter and carefully lift the salmon out of the baking dish and arrange it on top of the salsa (use 2 large spatulas to transfer it). Squeeze a few lime wedges over the fish and serve with additional lime wedges on the side.

grilled mahimahi with black bean salsa

SERVES 4

FOR THE MARINADE

½ cup soy sauce

½ cup fresh orange juice (from 1 large orange)

¼ cup ketchup

1 tablespoon honey

2 tablespoons lime juice

1 garlic clove, finely minced

1 teaspoon finely chopped fresh basil leaves

1 teaspoon finely chopped fresh oregano leaves

Freshly ground pepper

4 7- to 8-ounce mahimahi steaks, about 1 inch thick

FOR THE SALSA

2 cups cherry tomatoes, halved

2 scallions, white and light green parts only, thinly sliced

1 14-ounce can black beans, rinsed and drained

¼ cup chopped fresh cilantro leaves

1 jalapeño (seeded and ribbed for less heat), finely chopped

2 tablespoons lime juice

Salt

Canola or vegetable oil, for greasing the grill grates

Lime wedges, for serving

If the weather isn't cooperating and you can't grill outdoors, you can sear the mahimahi in a ridged grill pan. Heat a little oil in a skillet and cook over medium-high heat until both sides are browned and the fish is cooked through, about 5 minutes on each side.

1 To make the marinade, place the soy sauce, orange juice, ketchup, honey, lime juice, garlic, basil, oregano, and some pepper in a small bowl and whisk until the honey is completely dissolved. Pour the marinade into a resealable plastic bag with the fish fillets and refrigerate for 2 to 3 hours.

2 To make the salsa, toss the tomatoes, scallions, black beans, cilantro, jalapeño, and lime juice in a medium bowl. Add some salt to taste and set aside to let the flavors develop.

3 Preheat your grill to medium-high. Pour some oil into a small bowl. Using tongs, dip a wad of paper towels into the oil and use it to grease the grill grates. Grill the fish on each side without moving it until it is browned, firm, and flaky, 10 to 12 minutes total. Serve with the black bean salsa and lime wedges.

chica tip: Buy yourself a ridged grill pan and get perfect grill marks every time, rain or shine.

salmon pockets with yellow squash and cherry tomatoes

SERVES 4

2 yellow summer squash, sliced ½ inch thick

Salt and freshly ground pepper

4 6-ounce skinless salmon fillets

2 teaspoons dried oregano

1 pint cherry tomatoes, halved

4 scallions, light green and white parts only, sliced into 1-inch lengths

2 lemons, halved, plus lemon wedges for serving

chica tip: These "pockets" are yummy made with other kinds of fish and shellfish, too, and even meat, such as flank or skirt steak.

I love cooking in parchment packets. The fish cooks itself inside its neat parchment pouch, leaving behind no pans to clean. If you don't have parchment, aluminum foil will work just as well. Present each of your dinner guests with his or her own packet on a plate. Let them open the packet: The steam and perfume that are released are the best appeteaser ever.

1 Preheat your oven to 350°F.

2 Place four 16-inch-long rectangles of parchment paper on your work surface with the short side facing you. Crease each down the middle. Arrange some of the squash slices in a row, slightly overlapping, in the center of the bottom half of the rectangle. This will form the bed for your fish. Sprinkle the squash with some salt and pepper and then lay the salmon fillets on top. Season each fillet with ½ teaspoon of the oregano and salt and pepper to taste. Arrange some tomatoes and scallions on top of the fish, then squeeze the juice from ½ a lemon over each fillet.

3 Fold the parchment over the fish so that the top and bottom edges meet. Tightly crimp from one end around to the other and fold the edges of the parchment to seal the package. Place the packets on a rimmed baking sheet and bake for 10 to 12 minutes for 1-inch-thick fillets and 14 to 16 minutes for 1½-inch-thick fillets.

4 Remove the fish from the oven and carefully open the packets. Using a long, flat spatula, lift the fish out of the packet along with the squash and all of the toppings and place it on a plate. Drizzle with the packet juices and serve with a wedge of lemon on the side.

snapper pockets with
cilantro-lemongrass mojo

SERVES 4

5 4-inch lemongrass stalks, white bulb only, root end trimmed, outer layers peeled off, and stalk bruised with the back of a knife and thinly sliced

1 tightly packed cup fresh cilantro leaves

½ tightly packed cup fresh mint leaves, plus 2 tablespoons chopped mint for garnish

1 cup extra-virgin olive oil

2 garlic cloves, peeled

2 jalapeños, halved, seeded, and coarsely chopped

1 tablespoon paprika

1 teaspoon salt

2 tablespoons sherry vinegar

4 8-ounce skinless red snapper fillets, ¾ inch to 1 inch thick

Fish pockets are easy, easy, easy, and the fish is healthy, fragrant, and never dry. Rip the packets open to release an aromatic whiff of pure hunger-inducing temptation! Add some potatoes, asparagus, or zucchini for the easiest all-in-one supper ever. Mojo is an intensely garlicky marinade used in the Caribbean, as well as in many countries of Latin America. Because it is so acidic, you shouldn't let the fish marinate in the mojo for more than one hour or it will be "cooked" like ceviche. (See photo, page 104.)

1 Place the lemongrass, all but 2 tablespoons of the cilantro, the mint, ½ cup of the oil, the garlic, jalapeños, paprika, and salt in a food processor or blender and process until smooth. Add the remaining ½ cup of oil and the vinegar and process until smooth. Place the fish fillets in a large baking dish, cover with the mojo, and turn to coat. Cover with plastic wrap and refrigerate for up to 1 hour.

2 Preheat your oven to 350°F. Place four 16-inch-long rectangles of parchment paper on your work surface with the short side facing you. Crease each down the middle. Place a fillet in the center of the bottom half of the rectangle. Pour about ¼ cup of the mojo over each fillet and sprinkle with the remaining 2 tablespoons of cilantro. Fold the parchment over the fish so that the top and bottom edges meet. Tightly crimp from one end around to the other and fold the edges of the parchment to seal the package. Place the packets on a rimmed baking sheet and bake for 9 to 10 minutes for ¾-inch-thick fillets or up to 12 minutes for 1-inch-thick fillets.

3 Place the fish packets on a large serving dish and open the packets tableside. Serve the fish with juices from the packet and sprinkled with mint leaves.

dad's absolutely amazing brandied shrimp

SERVES 4

2 tablespoons unsalted butter

1 tablespoon olive oil

3 garlic cloves, finely minced

1 pound medium shrimp, peeled and deveined

2 teaspoons Worcestershire sauce

⅛ teaspoon Tabasco (or more to taste)

1 tablespoon chopped fresh oregano leaves

Salt and freshly ground pepper

½ cup ketchup

2 tablespoons brandy

3 tablespoons chopped fresh flat-leaf parsley

Que rico, **this is so tasty! If you like garlicky, buttery shrimp scampi, then you must try my dad's saucy, spicy brandied shrimp. For as long as I live, I'll be making this dish. My dad, who is an amazing cook, got the idea from a Colombian chef, and he, Mom, and I are always competing against one another to perfect it. Serve over pasta or white rice for a taste of heaven. Keep a bag of frozen shrimp in your freezer—they come in handy when you have no idea what to make for dinner! Place the sealed bag in a large bowl and defrost the shrimp under cold running water, or let them sit in a large bowl of cold water for a while—just remember to add more cold water every 20 minutes or so.**

1 Melt the butter with the olive oil in a large skillet over medium heat. Add the garlic and cook, stirring often, until it is fragrant, 1 to 2 minutes. Stir in the shrimp, Worcestershire sauce, Tabasco, oregano, and some salt and pepper and let the mixture simmer until the shrimp are partially cooked through and beginning to curl, about 2 minutes.

2 Stir in the ketchup and simmer until the shrimp are opaque and just cooked through, 2 more minutes. Add the brandy and parsley, stir to combine, remove from the heat, and serve.

chica tip: As a general rule, to avoid rubbery, over-cooked shrimp, don't cook them for more than 5 minutes total.

lemon-lime tilapia with melon salsa

SERVES 4

1 cup ½-inch cubes honeydew melon

1 mango, peeled, fruit cut off the seed (see page 50) and diced into ½-inch cubes (about 1 cup)

1 jalapeño, halved, seeded, and finely chopped

¼ cup lime juice (from about 2 limes)

¼ cup rice vinegar

¼ cup chopped fresh cilantro leaves

⅔ cup lemon juice (from about 2½ lemons)

2 teaspoons Delicioso Adobo Seasoning (page 22)

2 garlic cloves, finely minced

4 6-ounce tilapia fillets

1 tablespoon canola or vegetable oil

Tilapia is light and delicate tasting without much of a fishy flavor. The fillets are very thin, which is why you want to leave them alone once they hit the pan, otherwise they will fall apart. Adobo is my all-purpose seasoning; I use it on just about anything to give it a flavor boost. Make your own following the recipe on page 22; see "The Delicioso Pantry," page 10, for sources. It will keep for up to six months if stored in an airtight container in a dark, cool spot. Take any fruit left over from making the salsa and divide it into resealable freezer bags. Freeze and then use them in smoothies.

1 Place the melon, mango, jalapeño, lime juice, rice vinegar, and cilantro in a medium bowl. Stir to combine, cover with plastic wrap, and refrigerate for at least 1 hour or up to 1 day.

2 Whisk the lemon juice, ⅓ cup of water, the adobo, and the garlic together in a shallow dish. Add the tilapia and turn to coat. Cover with plastic wrap and refrigerate for at least 20 minutes or up to 1 hour.

3 Preheat your broiler to high. Line a baking sheet with aluminum foil and lightly grease with the oil. Remove the fish from the marinade and arrange the tilapia fillets on the baking sheet. Broil for about 8 minutes without turning, or until the fish is cooked through and flaky. Serve with the melon salsa.

tangy tomatillo shrimp

SERVES 4

3 tablespoons olive oil

1 pound (3 to 4) fresh poblano chiles, seeded, ribs removed, coarsely chopped

6 garlic cloves, finely minced

1 pound tomatillos, husked, rinsed, and quartered

1½ teaspoons salt, plus extra for the shrimp

3 tablespoons unsalted butter

2 pounds large shrimp, peeled and deveined

Freshly ground pepper

4 cups coarsely chopped fresh cilantro leaves

Whenever I travel, I try to take a cooking class in the town I am visiting, especially if I can find one taught by a casual, self-trained cook. I find that this relaxed style and practical approach to throwing food together better mirrors my own way of cooking and eating. I've taken classes from Napa to Paris and from Tuscany to Florida. I learned to make this Mexican-style shrimp while taking a class in Mexico City. It has a ton of cilantro, tangy tomatillos, and smoky poblano chiles, which adds up to a *muy delicioso* dish.

1 Heat the olive oil in a large skillet over medium-high heat for 1 minute. Add the chopped chiles and half of the garlic and cook until the chiles start to soften, about 5 minutes. Add the tomatillos and salt, reduce the heat to medium low, and cook, stirring occasionally, until the tomatillos begin to break down and release some liquid, about 10 minutes.

2 Transfer the tomatillo sauce to your blender, purée, and set aside.

3 Melt the butter in a large skillet over medium-high heat. Add the shrimp, season them with some salt and pepper, and toss in the remaining chopped garlic. Cook, stirring often, until the garlic becomes fragrant, 1 to 2 minutes. Add the tomatillo sauce and simmer until the shrimp are curled and opaque, 1 to 2 minutes more. Serve sprinkled with the cilantro.

pollo, every which way

though South American cuisine is perceived to be heavy on beef (because we raise the most delicious grass-fed beef in the world, if I do say so myself), you'll also often find chicken on our dinner plates.

Chicken is an important protein in South America; I could not imagine my life without Grandma Tita's chicken fricassee or my mother's arroz con pollo fantástico or her turkey during the holidays. In fact, South America has more *asaderos*—fast-food restaurants that specialize in grilled and rotisserie-cooked chicken—than we do burger shops. Come to think of it, didn't the Colonel come up with his "finger-licking good" slogan (*para chuparse los dedos*) after visiting Colombia and seeing the people thoroughly enjoy a bronzed, juicy chicken leg, licking every bit of chicken goodness from their fingers?

When I moved to the United States, I couldn't figure out why the chicken dishes I had made all the time at home, such as Lime and Rosemary Chicken or Pollo Pendejo, didn't taste the same. Where did all of the richness and sultry, deep flavors go? My mother, who moved to Miami after I did, had the same experience. It wasn't until I tried an organically raised chicken that my dishes came out tasting more like the food we ate at home. I don't buy organic chickens to be trendy or snobby. They really just taste better, and to me, flavor is worth a couple of extra dollars.

If you're a fan of boneless chicken cutlets, then you'll find lots of inspiration on these pages for ways to spice them up. Personally, I'm into legs; there's just something so deep-down good about eating a chicken leg with your fingers and nibbling off every little bit of meat, right down to the bone. If you are a leg person, too, then don't come to my house for dinner when I make a whole roast chicken unless you're ready to fight it out! May the hungriest *chica* or *chico* win.

chicken wings with mango-tamarind sauce

SERVES 4 TO 8

2 large mangos, peeled, fruit cut off of the seed and coarsely chopped (page 50)

1/3 cup dark brown sugar

2 teaspoons Worcestershire sauce

4 teaspoons tamarind paste (not tamarind pulp; see "The Delicioso Pantry," page 10)

1 teaspoon vegetable oil

1/2 teaspoon red pepper flakes

2 garlic cloves, coarsely chopped

2 pounds chicken wings, wing tips removed, or drumettes, rinsed and patted dry

Salt and freshly ground pepper

1 tablespoon canola or vegetable oil, for greasing the baking sheet

There is nothing better or more satisfying than getting down and dirty and eating with your hands, which is why I love chicken wings. Just make sure you choose your guest list wisely and invite the stuffy ones over another time and for another menu! Chicken wings are to be eaten with your closest friends; you know, the ones who won't mind seeing you lick your fingers! Tamarind pods are the fruit of a tree that grows in Asia and northern Africa. The paste, made from the pod's seeds, adds a fantastic tangy sweet-sour flavor to this sauce. You can find tamarind paste in many grocery stores, gourmet shops, and Asian and Indian markets.

1 Place the mangos, brown sugar, Worcestershire sauce, tamarind paste, oil, red pepper flakes, and garlic in a blender and purée until smooth.

2 Place the chicken wings in a large bowl and season with salt and pepper. Add just enough sauce to coat the wings (about 1/2 cup, reserve the rest) and toss to coat. Cover the chicken with plastic wrap and refrigerate for at least 30 minutes or up to 1 hour.

3 Preheat your oven to 400°F. Line a rimmed baking sheet with aluminum foil and grease the foil with the oil. Lift the chicken out of the sauce, letting the excess marinade drip back into the bowl. Place the wings on the prepared baking sheet and bake for 30 minutes, and then adjust a rack so it's 6 inches from the heating element, heat your broiler to high, and broil the wings for another 3 to 5 minutes, or until the sauce is sizzling.

4 While the wings bake, place the reserved sauce in a small saucepan and bring to a boil. Reduce the heat to medium low and simmer until syrupy, 5 to 10 minutes. Serve the chicken wings hot with the mango-tamarind sauce on the side for dipping.

chicken enchiladas
with fastest-ever salsa

SERVES 6

FOR THE SALSA

1 10-ounce can diced tomatoes with green chiles, drained

2 scallions, light green and white parts only, finely chopped

1 jalapeño, seeded, veined, and finely chopped (optional)

¼ cup finely chopped cilantro leaves

2 tablespoons lime juice (from about 1 lime)

Salt

FOR THE ENCHILADAS

1 tablespoon unsalted butter, softened

4 cups shredded rotisserie chicken or shredded from 2 pounds of cooked chicken breasts

12 ounces grated Cheddar cheese (about 2 cups)

2 cups sour cream

½ small red onion, finely chopped

Salt and freshly ground pepper

6 8-inch flour tortillas

Rotisserie-cooked chickens are one of the cook's best secret weapons ever. Whether I'm craving chicken soup, chicken salad, or these chicken enchiladas, starting with a whole roasted chicken lets me make it with very little effort. Leftover roast chicken also works well in this recipe. Even though this is perhaps the fastest-ever salsa, sometimes it's not fast enough—and that's when I use a jar of my favorite store-bought salsa instead!

1 To make the salsa, place the tomatoes, scallions, jalapeño (if using), cilantro, lime juice, and some salt in a medium bowl and stir to combine. Set aside at room temperature until ready to serve the enchiladas.

2 To make the enchiladas, preheat your oven to 350°F. Grease a 9 x 13-inch baking dish with the butter and set aside.

3 Place the chicken in a large bowl. Add 1½ cups of the grated cheese, the sour cream, red onion, and some salt and pepper. Mix well.

4 Place the tortillas on your work surface. Spoon about 1 cup of the chicken mixture onto the center of each tortilla and roll it up. Place the tortillas, seam side down, in the prepared baking dish (it will be a tight fit). Scatter the salsa over the tortillas. Cover with aluminum foil and bake until heated through, about 40 minutes.

5 Remove the foil and sprinkle the enchiladas with the remaining ½ cup of grated cheese. Return the baking dish to the oven until the cheese is melted and the edges of the tortillas are just beginning to get crisp, 5 to 8 minutes. Serve hot.

chicken breasts with guava and ginger

SERVES 4

⅔ cup guava jam or marmalade (not guava paste)

2 tablespoons lime juice (from about 1 lime)

1 tablespoon soy sauce

2 scallions, white and light green parts only, thinly sliced

½-inch piece of fresh ginger, peeled and grated

4 boneless, skinless chicken breast halves, trimmed of excess fat, rinsed and patted dry

1 tablespoon canola or vegetable oil, for greasing the broiler pan

Guava adds a wonderful sweetness and gorgeous color to this chicken dish. The flavor is exciting and exotic, and it really livens up chicken breast halves. Whether fresh, canned, or preserved as a marmalade or paste, guava is one of my favorite tropical fruits to play with. If you can't find guava jam or marmalade, use any sweet jam in its place, such as a mango or fig jam or a citrus marmalade.

1 Whisk the jam or marmalade, lime juice, soy sauce, scallions, and ginger together in a small saucepan over high heat. When it reaches a boil, transfer the mixture to a bowl and let it cool slightly.

2 Place the chicken in a large bowl and add 3 tablespoons of the guava marinade. Turn the chicken to coat, cover with plastic wrap, and marinate in your refrigerator for at least 30 minutes or up to 1 hour.

3 Preheat your oven to 350°F. Line the bottom of a broiler pan with aluminum foil and lightly grease the perforated top with the oil. Place the chicken on the oiled top and cover loosely with foil. Bake for about 15 minutes, then remove the foil and baste the chicken with the remaining guava marinade. Return to the oven, uncovered, and bake until the chicken is completely cooked through, 13 to 15 minutes. Remove from the oven and serve.

chica tip: The next time your market has a special on chicken breasts, buy a bunch to freeze. Wrap each chicken breast in freezer-safe plastic wrap (regular plastic wrap lets air get through) and freeze them flat on a baking sheet. Transfer the flat, frozen chicken to a freezer bag. Now you can defrost however many you need— from one to a few.

foolproof chicken (pollo pendejo)

SERVES 4 TO 6

3 tablespoons Delicioso Adobo Seasoning (page 22) or purchased adobo (see "The Delicioso Pantry," page 10)

3 tablespoons Worcestershire sauce

4 boneless, skinless chicken breast halves, trimmed of excess fat, rinsed and patted dry, and cut into 1 ½-inch chunks

1 tablespoon olive oil

4 tablespoons unsalted butter

1 medium yellow onion, halved and thinly sliced

2 garlic cloves, thinly sliced

1 cup light beer

1 8-ounce package sliced mushrooms

The literal translation of this dish is "idiot chicken," probably because it's really difficult to mess it up. Marinated and cooked in beer, the chicken is virtually guaranteed to come out moist and juicy, unless you really, really, *really* overcook it (if you're nervous about undercooked chicken, then insert a digital thermometer into the meatiest part of the cooked breast to make sure it reads 160°F. before serving). If you don't have any Worcestershire sauce around, try soy sauce instead. Serve this with buttered noodles or mashed potatoes.

1 Place the adobo and Worcestershire sauce in a gallon-size resealable plastic bag. Add the chicken and turn to coat. Refrigerate the chicken for at least 30 minutes or overnight.

2 Heat the oil and butter in a large skillet over medium-high heat. Once the butter has melted, add the onion and garlic. Reduce the heat to medium and cook, stirring occasionally, until the onion is soft and starts to brown, about 5 minutes.

3 Remove the chicken from the marinade and reserve the leftover marinating liquid. Pat the chicken dry with paper towels. Add the chicken to the skillet and cook until it is browned on all sides, about 10 minutes. Add the reserved marinating liquid, the beer, and the mushrooms; bring to a simmer and cook until the sauce is thick with a consistency like heavy cream, about 15 minutes. Remove from the heat and serve.

chica tip: When I buy chicken breasts in bulk to freeze, I always use a permanent marker to write the date that I bought the chicken on the bag, and I make sure to use the frozen chicken within a month or two.

peanut-crusted chicken breasts

SERVES 4

½ cup whole raw peanuts

¼ cup pumpkin seeds (pepitas)

1½ teaspoons ground coriander

1 teaspoon ground cumin

1 teaspoon smoked Spanish paprika (pimentón)

1 teaspoon dried thyme

1 teaspoon salt

½ teaspoon freshly ground pepper

2 eggs, lightly beaten

4 boneless, skinless chicken breasts, trimmed of excess fat, rinsed and patted dry

2 tablespoons olive oil

Crunchy and intensely flavorful, these chicken breasts are really, really *fantástico*. These are thick and juicy, but if you prefer thin cutlet-style chicken breasts, you can use them instead (they'll take about half as long to cook). They're excellent served solo, or with a dipping sauce on the side, such as an ají (see page 102), chimichurri (see page 162), or a quick chipotle mayo.

To make chipotle mayo, just chop up a chipotle chile from a can of chipotles en adobo and mix it, along with a teaspoon of the canned adobo sauce, into ¼ cup of mayonnaise. A squeeze of lime is a great finishing touch and adds a tangy counterpoint to the smoky chipotle.

Make a double batch of the cutlets—some for dinner tonight, and the rest for lunch on a roll with fresh cilantro and chipotle mayonnaise for tomorrow!

1 Preheat your oven to 350°F. Place the peanuts on a rimmed baking sheet and toast until they're barely golden, about 5 minutes, shaking the baking sheet midway through. Add the pumpkin seeds to the baking sheet and roast, shaking so the nuts brown evenly, until both the peanuts and the pumpkin seeds are lightly toasted, about 5 minutes. Remove from the oven and set aside until cooled completely.

2 Place the cooled peanuts and pumpkin seeds, the coriander, cumin, paprika, thyme, salt, and pepper into a spice mill, coffee grinder, or food processor, process until sandy (don't over-process into a paste), and transfer the mixture to a plate.

3 Pour the beaten eggs into a shallow dish. Dip each cutlet in the egg mixture and then dredge the cutlet through the peanut mixture, pressing it into the chicken so it adheres. Place the cutlets back on the plate, cover with plastic wrap, and refrigerate for 30 minutes.

4 Heat the olive oil in a large skillet over medium-high heat. Place the chicken breasts in the skillet and cook until they are golden brown on both sides, 12 to 16 minutes total. Remove from the heat and serve.

mushroom-stuffed chicken breasts with tomato-cumin sauce

SERVES 4

FOR THE SAUCE

1 28-ounce can diced tomatoes, drained

2 tablespoons red wine vinegar

2 garlic cloves, finely chopped

1 tablespoon tomato paste

1 teaspoon ground cumin

1½ teaspoons paprika

¼ cup olive oil

Salt and freshly ground pepper

Here's a technique that gives you a restaurant-ready presentation without a lot of effort. The thin chicken cutlet is rolled around a yummy mushroom stuffing and then tightly rolled in a sheet of plastic wrap, and then again in aluminum foil. Even after cooking and unwrapping, the chicken remains in a perfect cylinder, making the prettiest round medallions after slicing. Achiote is the turmeric of the Latin kitchen, and it adds a soft, musky flavor and intense color to foods like chicken and rice.

1 To make the sauce, place the tomatoes, vinegar, garlic, tomato paste, cumin, and paprika in a food processor and pulse until well combined. With the motor running, slowly add the olive oil in a thin stream and process until combined. Season to taste with salt and black pepper. Cover with plastic wrap and set aside on your counter or in the refrigerator.

2 To make the chicken, heat the olive oil in a large skillet over medium-high heat. Add the onion and garlic and cook, stirring occasionally, until the onion is softened and just starting to brown, about 5 minutes. Reduce the heat to medium low and add the mushrooms. Cook, stirring a couple of times, until the mushrooms release their moisture, about 10 minutes, then season with salt and pepper. Add the sherry, thyme, and coriander and continue to cook until the mixture is dry, another 5 minutes. Turn off the heat and set aside.

3 Place 1 chicken breast between two pieces of plastic wrap and, using a flat meat mallet or rolling pin, pound until the chicken is ¼ inch thick. Repeat with the other 3 breasts. Pat the chicken dry with paper towels and season both sides with salt and pepper. Sprinkle the skin side of the chicken evenly with ground achiote powder and turn it over (this will be the outside of the roll). Place 2 heaping tablespoons of the mushroom mixture in the center of the chicken breast and wrap the top and bottom flaps

FOR THE CHICKEN

2 tablespoons olive oil

½ small red onion, finely chopped

3 garlic cloves, finely minced

2 8-ounce packages sliced white button mushrooms (about 4 cups)

Salt and freshly ground pepper

1 tablespoon dry sherry

½ teaspoon dried thyme or 1 teaspoon chopped fresh thyme leaves

½ teaspoon ground coriander

4 boneless, skinless chicken breast halves, tenderloin removed (reserve for another use) and trimmed of excess fat

2 teaspoons achiote powder

Thyme sprigs, for garnish

tightly around the filling. Fold the sides around to make a nice little package. Tightly wrap the stuffed breast in a 12 x 18-inch sheet of plastic wrap, twisting the ends like a candy wrapper. Knot the ends and wrap the roll in a sheet of aluminum foil. Repeat with the remaining breasts and filling.

4 Bring a large pot of water to a boil. Add the chicken packages and reduce the heat to medium low. Simmer the chicken for 18 minutes. Carefully remove the rolls from the water and set aside to cool slightly.

5 While the chicken cools, place the tomato-cumin sauce in a small saucepan over medium-high heat to warm through. Using kitchen shears, cut the ends off of the foil packets and carefully remove the foil and plastic from each rolled breast (use tongs if it's still hot). Slice each breast into ½-inch discs. Place the sliced rounds on a plate, drizzle with some sauce, and serve.

rum chica rum chicken

SERVES 4 TO 6

⅔ cup dark rum

⅓ cup fresh orange juice plus 1 teaspoon orange zest and 1 orange, thinly sliced into rounds, for garnish

3 tablespoons Worcestershire sauce

1-inch piece of fresh ginger, peeled and grated

2 tablespoons dark brown sugar

6 garlic cloves, finely chopped

¼ cup chopped fresh cilantro leaves

2 pounds boneless, skinless chicken breasts or thighs, trimmed of excess fat, rinsed and patted dry

I often serve chicken for parties, and Rum Chica Rum Chicken is fun, inexpensive, and a perennial crowd pleaser. Grill, broil, or pan-sear (with a little oil) some fresh pineapple slices and then toss them with lime juice, sliced jalapeños, and a drizzle of oil for a fantastic topper. If the weather isn't good for grilling, go ahead and cook the chicken under your broiler or sear it in a skillet.

1 Whisk the rum, orange juice, orange zest, Worcestershire sauce, ginger, brown sugar, garlic, and 2 tablespoons of the cilantro together in a large bowl. Add the chicken pieces, cover with plastic wrap, and refrigerate for at least 30 minutes or up to 4 hours.

2 Preheat your grill to medium hot. Remove the chicken from the marinade, reserving the marinade, and shake off any solids. Cook the chicken until it is browned on both sides and the juices run clear, about 10 minutes per side, basting with the leftover marinade a few times throughout. (For safety, don't baste again once the chicken has been turned a final time, as the marinade will not be sufficiently cooked.) Serve sprinkled with the remaining 2 tablespoons of cilantro and garnish with the orange slices.

lime chicken with quick avocado salsa

SERVES 4

FOR THE SALSA

2 medium tomatoes, cored, halved, and chopped

½ white onion, finely chopped

1 cup coarsely chopped fresh cilantro leaves

2 tablespoons white vinegar

Salt and freshly ground pepper

3 medium Hass avocados, halved, pitted, peeled, and coarsely chopped

FOR THE CHICKEN

4 tablespoons (½ stick) unsalted butter

8 boneless, skinless chicken thighs, trimmed of excess fat, rinsed and patted dry

1 teaspoon salt

1 teaspoon freshly ground pepper

½ teaspoon paprika

1 large yellow onion, thinly sliced

1 garlic clove, finely minced

⅓ cup lime juice (from about 3 limes), plus lime wedges for serving

Dark meat is moister than white meat and can stand up to strong acids such as lime juice. If your market doesn't have boneless thighs, you can cook this with bone-in thighs instead (or bone the thighs yourself). The texture of the salsa is a bit chunky and makes for a good contrast between the creamy avocado and the chicken.

1 To make the salsa, stir the tomatoes, onion, cilantro, vinegar, and salt and pepper together in a large bowl. Add the avocados, toss gently to combine, and set aside.

2 To make the chicken, melt the butter in a large skillet over medium-high heat. Add the chicken and cook until it is browned on all sides, about 8 minutes. Sprinkle the salt, pepper, and paprika over the chicken. Add the onion and garlic and continue to cook, stirring occasionally, until the onion is soft, about 5 minutes.

3 Add the lime juice to the skillet and bring it to a simmer. Cover the skillet and simmer until the chicken is cooked through, 15 to 20 minutes. Serve with the avocado salsa and lime wedges

chica tip: Our grandmas might have left frozen chicken on the counter to defrost, but with the risk of bacterial contamination in today's chickens (yes, even in organically raised chickens), it's too dangerous. Instead, defrost frozen chicken overnight in your fridge; defrost it in a big bowl of cold water (changing the water every 30 minutes until the chicken is thawed); or defrost it in your microwave, following the manufacturer's instructions.

arroz con pollo

SERVES 4 TO 6

1 3- to 4-pound chicken, cut in 8 serving pieces, rinsed and patted dry

1 medium yellow onion, quartered, plus ½ yellow onion, thinly sliced

4 cups homemade or canned low-sodium chicken broth

1 cup light beer, such as lager

3 tablespoons Delicioso Adobo Seasoning (page 22) or purchased adobo (see "The Delicioso Pantry," page 10)

3 tablespoons Worcestershire sauce

1 cup chopped fresh cilantro leaves

6 garlic cloves, coarsely chopped

3 cups white rice

1 cup fresh or frozen peas

2 medium carrots, finely diced

8 ounces green beans, trimmed and quartered

1 cup ketchup

1 teaspoon salt

3 tablespoons unsalted butter

½ red bell pepper, cored, seeded, ribbed, and thinly sliced

½ green bell pepper, cored, seeded, ribbed, and thinly sliced

1 cup pimento-stuffed olives

I grew up eating arroz con pollo at least once a week, and I learned how to make it by standing at my mom's side. Now my friends beg me to make it for them. It's especially great served for late-afternoon weekend lunches with big groups of friends. Add some sangria and plantain chips (page 203) and you're as close to heaven as you can get. No one ever leaves even the smallest crumb on their plates, and everyone helps themselves to seconds, so if you want leftovers, you'd better hide the pot! If you need your arroz con pollo fix fast, use frozen mixed peas and carrots and frozen green beans instead of fresh. Add the carrots and green beans along with the peas and chicken broth.

1 Place the chicken, quartered onion, 1 cup of the chicken broth, the beer, adobo, Worcestershire sauce, half of the cilantro, and the garlic in a large pot or skillet over high heat. Bring to a boil, reduce the heat to medium low, cover, and simmer until the chicken is cooked through, 30 to 35 minutes. Remove the chicken to a plate and set aside to cool; once it is cool, remove the meat from the bones, shred it, and set aside. Discard the skin and bones. Strain the broth into a bowl through a fine-mesh sieve, discarding the onion pieces.

2 Pour the broth into a measuring cup and add enough of the remaining 3 cups of chicken broth to equal 4 cups. Return it to the pot or skillet and add the rice, peas, carrots, green beans, ketchup, and salt. Stir well and bring to a boil. Let the liquid evaporate to just below the level of the rice, about 10 minutes, and then reduce the heat to low, cover, and cook until the rice is tender and fully cooked, about 25 minutes.

3 Meanwhile, melt the butter in a large skillet over medium heat. Add the bell peppers and the sliced onions and cook until they're tender, about 8 minutes. Add the shredded chicken to the vegetables. Cook until it is heated through, 2 to 3 minutes. Fluff the rice with a fork and add the chicken and vegetables to the rice mixture. Stir in the olives, sprinkle with the remaining cilantro, and serve.

grandma tita's chicken fricassee

SERVES 4

8 ounces fresh white or green asparagus, stalks trimmed and sliced into 1-inch lengths

4 skin-on, bone-in chicken breast halves, trimmed of excess fat, rinsed and patted dry

1 cup homemade or canned low-sodium chicken broth

1 large white onion, finely chopped

4 garlic cloves, minced

2 tablespoons Worcestershire sauce

1 teaspoon grated lemon zest

1 teaspoon ground cumin

1 teaspoon dried oregano

1 teaspoon salt

½ teaspoon freshly ground pepper

⅓ cup all-purpose flour

⅓ cup heavy cream

¼ cup strained brine-packed capers

White rice, for serving

My grandma Tita was quite a character. In the 1960s, she was the Colombian ambassador to Germany, and she lived abroad for years. When we went to visit her, we would eat dinner in her very serious dining room with lots of silverware and a long table, right out of the movies, that could seat twenty-four people! She loved to eat and, like most women in my family, had the appetite of a truck driver.

1 Bring a large pot of salted water to a boil. Add the asparagus and cook until tender, 5 to 8 minutes. Reserve ¾ cup of the cooking liquid and then strain the asparagus. Rinse under cold water and transfer to a paper-towel-lined plate. Set aside.

2 Place the chicken breasts in a large pot with the chicken broth, onion, garlic, Worcestershire sauce, lemon zest, cumin, oregano, salt, and pepper. Cover, bring to a boil, then reduce the heat to medium low and simmer until the chicken is cooked through, about 15 minutes. Transfer the chicken to a plate, then strain the broth through a fine-mesh sieve and set it aside until cooled. Remove the chicken from the bones, discarding the skin and pulling the meat off in big, long chunks.

3 Place the flour in a large bowl. Add a little of the chicken's cooking broth to the flour, whisking it until it forms a smooth paste. Whisk in the remaining broth, then pour the mixture into a medium saucepan. Bring the sauce to a simmer over medium heat, stirring constantly so it doesn't stick or burn, until it has thickened slightly, about 15 minutes.

4 Whisk in the reserved asparagus cooking liquid, the cream, and the capers. Add the chicken back to the sauce and stir to coat in the sauce. Add the asparagus and gently tuck it into the sauce (the asparagus is very delicate, so handle it carefully). Cook for a couple of minutes to heat through and bring the flavors together, and serve with rice.

lime and rosemary chicken

SERVES 4

5 medium yellow onions (about 2 pounds), unpeeled and quartered

2 tablespoons olive oil

Salt and freshly ground pepper

4 garlic cloves, thinly sliced

1 lemon, halved and thinly sliced

1 lime, halved and thinly sliced

3-pound chicken, rinsed inside and out and patted dry

1 tablespoon chopped fresh rosemary, plus 2 extra sprigs

2 tablespoons Delicioso Adobo Seasoning (page 22) or purchased adobo (see "The Delicioso Pantry," page 10)

Nothing smells better than a chicken roasting in the oven. Make this simple recipe when you crave something warm and comforting, or when you want to make friends or houseguests feel welcome from the second they walk through the door. When you bring it to the table, the herbs and little bits of lime will be seductively visible through the crisp chicken skin.

1 Preheat your oven to 400°F. Line a roasting pan or a rimmed baking sheet with aluminum foil and set aside.

2 Place the onions in a large bowl. Add the olive oil, some salt and pepper, a pinch of the garlic slices, and a few lemon and lime slices. Toss to coat, place the mixture in the bottom of the prepared pan, and set aside.

3 Trim any excess fat off of the chicken and tuck its wings underneath its back. Using your fingers, gently separate the skin from the breasts, legs, and thighs. Rub a pinch of rosemary on the meat under the skin of the breast and then stuff a few slices of the garlic, lemon, and lime beneath the chicken's skin. Continue seasoning the thigh and leg meat, using the rest of the herbs, garlic, lemon, and lime.

4 Rub the chicken, inside and out, with the adobo. Tie the chicken's legs together with kitchen twine and place the chicken on a rack set over the onion mixture on the prepared pan.

5 Roast the chicken, basting it with pan drippings occasionally, until the juices at the leg-thigh joint run clear and a digital thermometer inserted in the thickest part of the thigh reads 165°F, 1 hour to 1 hour and 20 minutes, stirring the onions midway through cooking (if at any time the onions look to be browning too much, add ½ cup of water to the roasting pan or baking sheet). Transfer the chicken to a cutting board, loosely tent it with aluminum foil, and transfer the onions to a serving platter. When the chicken has rested for 10 minutes, remove the lemon and lime slices, carve it, and arrange it on a platter with the onions.

easy turkey hash (picadillo)

SERVES 4

2 tablespoons olive oil

1 yellow onion, chopped

1 red bell pepper, cored, seeded, ribbed, and chopped

1 garlic clove, finely minced

2 pounds ground turkey

1½ cups ketchup

¼ cup chopped raisins

3 tablespoons Worcestershire sauce

2 tablespoons dark brown sugar

1 tablespoon white wine vinegar

1 teaspoon fresh lemon juice

1 teaspoon paprika

1 teaspoon salt

¼ cup chopped pitted green olives

Every Latin American country makes its own version of picadillo, a hash made most often from beef. I thought it might be good made with lean ground turkey, and boy, was I right! With a texture almost like a bolognese sauce, it's really great served over pasta, polenta, or even a side of mashed potatoes for a south-of-the-border Thanksgiving flavor. Picadillo is also great with tortillas, arepas, or rice, or you can stuff it into peppers, zucchini, or eggplant.

1 Heat the oil in a large skillet over medium-high heat. Add the onion, bell pepper, and garlic and cook, stirring often, until the vegetables are soft but not browned, 3 to 5 minutes. Add the turkey meat and cook, stirring often, until it is no longer pink, about 5 minutes. Stir in the ketchup, raisins, Worcestershire sauce, brown sugar, vinegar, lemon juice, paprika, and salt. Reduce the heat to medium low, cover, and simmer until all of the flavors come together and the meat is well crumbled and separated, 10 minutes. Stir in the green olives and serve.

TURKEY PICADILLO MELTS These are great served as starters in individual ramekins. Line four 3-inch ramekins with a few thin slices of Gouda cheese, so that half of each cheese slice hangs over the rim of the ramekin. Fill the cup with some hash and then fold the cheese over the filling. Bake at 350°F. until the cheese is melted and browned around the edges, about 30 minutes. Serve immediately with toast.

mom's holiday turkey with stuffing and lime-cranberry sauce

SERVES 12 TO 14

FOR THE MARINADE

1 large yellow onion, coarsely chopped

6 garlic cloves, coarsely chopped

1 cup yellow mustard

½ cup Worcestershire sauce

1 16- to 18-pound turkey, gizzard reserved and chopped

FOR THE LIME-CRANBERRY SAUCE

2 12-ounce bags fresh cranberries, washed

3 cups sugar

2 cups fresh orange juice (from about 8 oranges) plus 1 tablespoon grated orange zest

½ cup lime juice (from about 4 limes)

FOR THE STUFFING

10 large eggs

1 cup (2 sticks) unsalted butter

1½ pounds lean ground beef (ground 3 times)

1½ pounds ground pork (ground 3 times)

I don't care what anyone says, this is, and always will be, the best turkey and stuffing anywhere in the world! When we were kids, Mom only made her famous bird to celebrate Christmas, but once we moved to Miami, we were lucky enough to have it for Thanksgiving, too. I just couldn't imagine a winter holiday without these dishes.

Mom always grinds her meat a couple of extra times so the stuffing isn't too grainy. If you don't have a meat grinder at home, become friends with the butcher at your grocery store and ask him or her to run the meat through the grinder a few extra times for you. The marinade can be made the night before you plan on roasting the turkey. If you have leftover stuffing after filling the bird, place it in a butter casserole dish and bake it once the bird comes out of the oven. Serve alongside the rest of the spread; you can never have too much stuffing!

1 To make the marinade, place the onion, garlic, mustard, and Worcestershire sauce in your food processor and purée. Rub the turkey, inside and out, with the mixture. Place it in a large roasting pan and cover with plastic wrap. Refrigerate the turkey overnight or up to 24 hours.

2 To make the sauce, bring the cranberries, sugar, orange juice and zest, and lime juice to a boil in a large saucepan over medium-high heat. Reduce the heat to low and simmer until the sauce is thick and the cranberries have broken down, 15 to 20 minutes. Transfer to a serving dish and let the cranberry sauce cool. Cover with plastic wrap and refrigerate until you're ready to serve.

3 To make the stuffing, Place the eggs in a large saucepan and cover them with water. Bring the water to a boil, cover, and turn off the heat. Let the eggs sit for 10 minutes. Set aside to cool completely before peeling and chopping. *(recipe continues)*

3 large yellow onions, finely chopped

15 garlic cloves, finely chopped

1 cup steak sauce

½ cup apple cider vinegar

1 tablespoon lemon zest

1 tablespoon ground cumin

1 tablespoon dried oregano

1 tablespoon salt

1½ teaspoons freshly ground pepper

5 slices of white bread

3 tablespoons milk

1 red bell pepper, cored, seeded, ribbed, and finely chopped

1 green bell pepper, cored, seeded, ribbed, and finely chopped

5 celery stalks, thinly sliced

20 scallions, white and light green parts only, finely chopped (about 1½ cups)

4 ounces tomato paste

1 pound cooked sausage, sliced

1 cup raisins

1 cup finely chopped fresh flat-leaf parsley leaves

7-ounce bottle pimento-stuffed olives, sliced

2 bottles dark malt beverage (such as Malta)

4 Melt ½ cup (1 stick) of the butter in a large pot over medium-high heat. Add the beef, pork, and the reserved chopped gizzards and cook until the meat is starting to brown, 8 to 10 minutes. Add ½ cup of the chopped onions and half of the chopped garlic, along with the steak sauce, vinegar, lemon zest, cumin, oregano, salt, and pepper. Cook, stirring often, until the onions are completely tender and the meat is cooked through, 35 to 45 minutes. Turn off the heat and let the mixture cool. Cover with plastic wrap and refrigerate until you're ready to make the rest of the stuffing (the meat base can be made up to 1 day in advance).

5 Soak the bread in the milk for 3 minutes. Squeeze as much liquid from the bread as you can and then crumble it into a small bowl and set aside.

6 Melt the remaining ½ cup (1 stick) of butter in a large pot over medium-high heat. Stir in the remaining onions and garlic along with the bell peppers, celery, and scallions. Add the tomato paste and cook until the liquid in the pot is nearly evaporated, about 15 minutes. Add the meat mixture, crumbled bread, chopped eggs, sausage, raisins, parsley, and stuffed olives and mix to combine. Let the stuffing cool completely before stuffing the turkey.

7 Preheat your oven to 300°F.

8 Fill the cavity and the neck of the turkey with the stuffing. Tuck the turkey wings beneath the breast and tie the base of the legs together with kitchen twine. Using a pastry brush or bulb baster, baste the turkey with some of the malt and then roast, covered with aluminum foil, for 2 hours, basting every 30 minutes with the malt. Increase the oven temperature to 350°F. and uncover the turkey (save the foil). Continue to roast for another 2 to 3 hours, basting the turkey every 30 minutes, until the juices run clear and the turkey's temperature at the thickest part of the leg reads 175°F, on a digital thermometer. If the turkey breast ever starts to look like it's getting too dark, cover it with aluminum foil.

9 Remove the turkey from the oven and cover it loosely with the reserved foil. Let the turkey rest for 30 minutes before carving and serving with the stuffing on the side.

chipotle tamale pie

SERVES 6

1 tablespoon unsalted butter, at room temperature

1 tablespoon olive oil

¾ pound ground turkey (preferably white meat) or lean ground beef

1 medium yellow onion, chopped

1 green bell pepper, cored, seeded, ribbed, and diced

2 garlic cloves, finely minced

Salt and freshly ground pepper

2 teaspoons ground cumin

1 15-ounce can pinto beans, rinsed and drained

1 8-ounce can diced tomatoes

1 to 2 canned chipotle chiles en adobo, seeded and minced, plus 1 teaspoon adobo sauce

1 cup grated Cheddar cheese

½ cup chopped fresh cilantro leaves

1 8.5-ounce package corn bread mix (plus ingredients needed to make the corn bread batter)

If a Mexican and a Southerner got in the kitchen to cook side by side, this is the kind of food that I think they would make: comforting, spicy, and generous enough to feed an army of friends or family. Tamale pie is like corn bread and chili in one —and it's really satisfying. Kids love this dish, but you might want to omit the chipotle chile if making it for young taste buds!

1 Preheat your oven to 400°F. Grease an 8-inch square baking dish with the butter and set it aside.

2 Heat the olive oil in a nonstick skillet over medium heat. Add the ground turkey, onion, bell pepper, and garlic, season with salt and pepper, and cook until the turkey is no longer pink and is cooked through, about 8 minutes. Drain off any excess fat and sprinkle the meat mixture with the cumin.

3 Add the beans, tomatoes, chiles, and adobo sauce to the skillet and bring to a boil over high heat. Reduce the heat to medium and simmer until heated through and slightly thickened, 5 minutes. Remove the pan from the heat and stir in the cheese and cilantro.

4 Spread the turkey mixture in the prepared baking dish, pressing down on it with the back of a spoon to make an even, compact layer.

5 Prepare the corn bread mix according to the manufacturer's instructions. Spread the corn bread batter over the turkey mixture and bake until the corn bread is golden brown, 20 to 25 minutes. Let the tamale pie stand for 5 minutes before cutting into squares and serving.

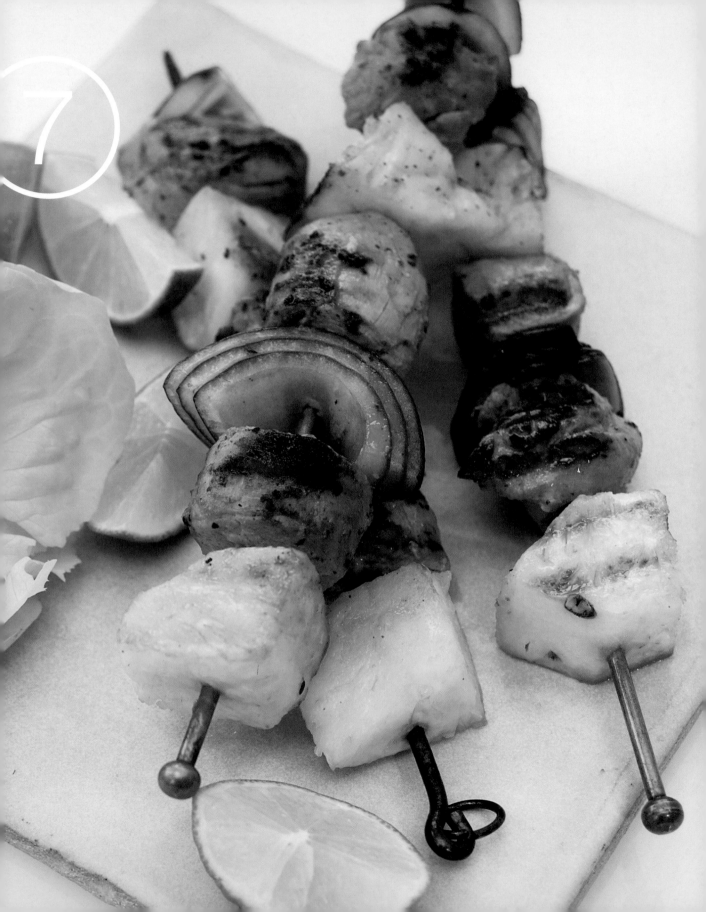

carne knowledge

I am a real *Latinaza*; I love all kinds of meat, from steaks and chops to shredded, roasted, and stewed, on the bone and off, grilled and pan-fried.

A few years ago I found myself needing a break from the frantic activity of my daily life. Yoga and meditation helped me find some time to be silent and quiet my thoughts. I took to it immediately—up to a point. In order to *really* purify my mind, body, and soul, my instructor told me to abstain from physical relationships, forgo alcohol, and give up eating meat. Since the first two were out of the question, no meat it would be. That's how this *carne*-loving *chica* became a vegetarian.

I lasted four and a half days. Just the thought of never again tasting ribs, steaks, chicken wings, or chops left me in such a state that I couldn't eat, drink, sleep, or meditate. I realized that life is too short to sacrifice some of my favorite foods. Instead I decided to embrace my *amor carnal* responsibly, by recycling, by purchasing organically or humanely raised meats, and by advocating for better lives for the animals that are a part of our food chain.

On my journey to becoming a more informed consumer, I made friends with the butchers at my supermarket. It's amazing how with just a little effort, your butcher can become one of your best assets. I take them little Christmas gifts and always stop to chat with them. In return, I get above-and-beyond service, the best cuts of meat, and answers to all of my questions.

I also learned to pay attention to product labels and to terms like *grass-fed, organic, humanely raised,* and *antibiotic-free.* All it takes is a little extra effort to find bacon and ham free of sulfites and other preservatives. Yes, it does cost extra to eat with compassion, but my appetite is the better for it.

grilled pork and pineapple skewers
with achiote sauce

SERVES 4

3 tablespoons canola or vegetable oil

1 tablespoon achiote (annatto) seeds

½ cup red wine vinegar

5 garlic cloves, finely minced

1 tablespoon seeded and finely chopped canned ají amarillo peppers (or 1 tablespoon finely chopped roasted red or yellow peppers plus ¼ teaspoon cayenne pepper)

2 teaspoons ground cumin

2 teaspoons salt, plus extra for the skewers

2 teaspoons freshly ground pepper, plus extra for the skewers

1 pound pork loin, cut into 1-inch cubes

1 pineapple, peeled, cored, and cut into 1-inch cubes

1 large red onion, quartered, then halved widthwise

1 head of butterhead lettuce (such as Bibb or Boston)

Lime wedges, for serving

This is a great dish to serve at a barbecue or garden party. The lettuce leaves serve two purposes: They make this simple barbecue dish look really elegant, and they can be used to wrap around the de-skewered pork and pineapple chunks—kind of like a lettuce-leaf taco. You can use metal or wooden skewers; if using wooden ones, make sure to soak them in water for a few hours before using so they don't burn on the grill. I absolutely love ají amarillo, yellow Peruvian peppers (see "The Delicioso Pantry," page 10), but if you don't have any, you can use roasted red bell peppers with a dash of cayenne. If the weather isn't cooperating, use a ridged grill pan or a skillet to cook the pork and sear the onion and pineapple.

1 Heat the oil in a small saucepan over medium-high heat and add the achiote seeds. Turn off the heat and let the seeds steep until the oil turns a vibrant orange-red, about 5 minutes. Strain the oil through a fine-mesh sieve and discard the seeds. Place the achiote oil in a blender along with the vinegar, garlic, ají amarillo, cumin, salt, and pepper and purée the mixture.

2 Place the pork in a resealable gallon-size plastic bag. Add the achiote marinade, turn the bag to coat the pork, and refrigerate for at least 4 hours or overnight.

3 Preheat your grill to high. Thread the pork onto skewers alternately with the pineapple and red onion. Sprinkle the skewers with a little salt and pepper. Grill until browned on all sides, 4 to 6 minutes total; don't overcook or the pork will be tough and dry. Serve the skewers on a bed of lettuce leaves with some lime wedges.

pork cutlets with mango-rum chutney (empanizados)

SERVES 4

FOR THE MARINADE

1 yellow onion, chopped

4 garlic cloves, finely minced

½ cup sour orange juice (see headnote)

1 teaspoon plus a pinch of salt

8 thin pork loin cutlets

FOR THE CHUTNEY

¾ cup white vinegar

¼ cup spiced rum

½ cup golden raisins

½ cup dark brown sugar

1 red onion, chopped

½ yellow bell pepper, cored, seeded, ribbed, and chopped

2-inch piece of fresh ginger, peeled and finely chopped

1 garlic clove, finely minced

1 teaspoon ground allspice

2 large mangos, peeled and cubed (see page 50)

1 green apple, peeled, halved, cored, and cubed

4 large eggs

2 cups dry or freshly made bread crumbs

Olive oil, for frying

This is the Latin version of schnitzel or cutlets Milanese. Marinating the pork cutlets overnight gives them lots of flavor, and the chutney adds an extra boost, too. You can make the chutney up to one week ahead of time and serve any leftovers with chicken or roasted pork or on a turkey sandwich. It's nice to make some for friends, too, or pack it in a nice jar, tie with raffia, and offer it as a hostess gift. Bottles of sour orange juice can be found in most supermarkets, or substitute 3 tablespoons plus 1 teaspoon of orange juice and 2 teaspoons of lime juice.

1 To make the marinade, place the onion, garlic, orange juice, and 1 teaspoon salt in a resealable gallon-size plastic bag. Add the pork, turn to coat, and refrigerate overnight.

2 Meanwhile, make the chutney. Stir the vinegar, rum, raisins, brown sugar, red onion, bell pepper, ginger, garlic, and allspice together in a medium saucepan over medium-high heat. Bring to a boil, stirring occasionally. Reduce the heat to medium low and simmer until the onion and pepper are soft, 8 to 10 minutes. Add the mangos and the apple and continue to simmer, stirring occasionally, until the fruit begins to break down and the mixture is thick and jammy, 15 to 25 minutes. Turn off the heat and set aside to cool. Cover and refrigerate for up to 1 week.

3 Beat the eggs with a pinch of salt in a shallow dish and place the bread crumbs on a plate. Heat the oil in a large skillet over medium-high heat until very hot. Dip the marinated pork into the beaten egg, letting the excess drip off, and then into the bread crumbs, pressing the pork into the bread crumbs to evenly coat both sides. Reduce the heat to medium and fry the cutlets until they are golden brown, 2 to 4 minutes on each side. Transfer to a paper-towel-lined plate to drain and serve with the chutney.

cumin-broiled pork chops

SERVES 4

½ cup soy sauce

1 teaspoon ground cumin

½ teaspoon freshly ground black pepper

¼ teaspoon cayenne pepper

¼ teaspoon ground cinnamon

¼ teaspoon ground cloves

¼ cup plus 1 tablespoon olive oil

1 large yellow onion, chopped

2 garlic cloves, coarsely chopped

4 1-inch-thick pork loin chops

Soy sauce adds a great, earthy flavor to these chops and works with the other big flavors—the cooked and puréed onions, garlic, and spices—to quickly penetrate the meat, infusing it with tons of flavor in just one hour. This marinade is excellent for flavoring flank steak and chicken breasts.

1 Whisk the soy sauce with the cumin, black pepper, cayenne, cinnamon, and cloves in a small bowl and set aside.

2 Heat 1 tablespoon of the olive oil in a large skillet over medium-high heat for 1 minute. Add the onion and garlic and cook, stirring occasionally, until the onion is soft, about 2 minutes. Add the onion and garlic to the soy sauce mixture and then transfer all of it to a food processor and pulse until smooth. With the motor running, slowly add the remaining ¼ cup of olive oil.

3 Place the pork chops in a gallon-size resealable plastic bag with two-thirds of the marinade (reserve the rest). Marinate in your refrigerator for up to an hour.

4 Heat your broiler to high. Remove the pork chops from the marinade (discard the marinade) and pat them dry with paper towels. Place the chops on an aluminum-foil-lined broiler pan. Broil until each side is browned and the chops are cooked through, 8 to 10 minutes per side, basting occasionally with the reserved marinade.

chica tip: To avoid heavy-duty scrubbing, liberally spray a baking dish, sheet pan, or broiler pan inside and out with pan spray before using. I even spray the handles (note that you have to be a little more careful when handling the pan so you don't lose your grip).

coffee and cola pork loin

SERVES 4 TO 6

FOR THE PORK LOIN

1 cup warm water

1 cup apple cider vinegar

¼ cup sugar

2 tablespoons salt

1 2½- to 3-pound pork loin

¼ cup ground coffee beans

3 tablespoons dark brown sugar

2 tablespoons whole peppercorns

3 whole star anise

1 ½-inch piece of cinnamon stick, broken into small pieces

3 tablespoons unsalted butter

3 tablespoons canola or vegetable oil

FOR THE SAUCE

1 cup pineapple juice

2 tablespoons cornstarch

1 cup dark brown sugar

2 cups cola

2 tablespoons lime juice (from about 1 lime)

This recipe is a tribute to my grandparents. One of my strongest early memories is of the aroma of strong black coffee that filled my grandparents' home. They would drink coffee while I sipped a Coke; my grandfather worked for Coca-Cola for a while, so he always had a ton of Coke in the house. I put the two together and came up with this recipe for pork loin. To play off of the coffee's bitterness and the cola's sweetness, I add star anise, cinnamon, and lots of coarsely ground peppercorns. Brining the pork overnight makes it extra juicy, tender, and flavorful.

1 To make the pork, combine the warm water with the vinegar, sugar, and salt in a medium bowl, whisking until the sugar and salt are dissolved. Transfer to a resealable gallon-size plastic bag. Add 1 cup of cold water and the pork loin, seal, and refrigerate overnight.

2 Pulse the coffee, brown sugar, peppercorns, star anise, and cinnamon stick in a coffee or spice grinder until they are a fine powder. Remove the pork loin from the brine and pat dry with paper towels. Rub the pork with the spice mix, transfer to a baking sheet lined with aluminum foil, and set it aside at room temperature.

3 Preheat your oven to 350°F. In a large skillet, melt the butter with the oil over medium-high heat. Add the pork loin and brown for 5 minutes, turning to brown all sides. Return the pork to the baking sheet and roast until its temperature reads 160°F. on a digital thermometer, about 1 hour. Remove the roast from the oven, cover loosely with aluminum foil, and let it rest for 10 minutes before slicing.

4 While the pork roasts, make the sauce. Place the pineapple juice and cornstarch in a medium saucepan and whisk together. Turn the heat on to medium high and add the brown sugar, cola, and lime juice, whisking until the sugar has dissolved. Bring back to a simmer over medium-high heat for 5 minutes, whisking occasionally, until the sauce is thick like heavy cream. Slice the pork loin and serve with the sauce on the side.

tamarind-glazed baby back ribs

SERVES 4 TO 6

2 racks of baby back pork ribs (about 2 pounds each)

Salt and freshly ground pepper

2 ají panca or ancho chiles, soaked in hot water

½ cup tamarind paste (see "The Delicioso Pantry," page 10)

3 to 4 tablespoons light or dark brown sugar

2 tablespoons Worcestershire sauce

⅓ cup lemon juice (from about 1 lemon)

½ cup orange juice (preferably freshly squeezed from about ½ orange)

4 garlic cloves, coarsely chopped

chica tip: Setting aside a small portion of the glaze for brushing over the cooked ribs just before serving ensures that you won't eat sauce that has made contact with raw or undercooked pork.

Sticky, sweet, and totally yummylicious, these ribs are a great excuse to get messy and eat with your hands. Make them for a Fourth of July party and you'll be an instant hit! Hide some for leftovers later at night; for some reason, ribs always taste best cold or as a midnight snack! Ají panca is a wonderfully mild dried Peruvian chile pepper with a sweet, berry-like fruity flavor that works really well with pork. See "The Delicioso Pantry," page 10, or replace it with another mild dried chile.

1 Preheat your oven to 300°F.

2 Sprinkle the ribs with salt and pepper and place them meaty side up on an aluminum-foil-lined rimmed baking sheet or shallow baking dish. Roast for 30 minutes and then drain off any accumulated fat from the baking sheet. Turn the ribs over and increase the oven temperature to 400°F. Return them to the oven for an additional 30 minutes.

3 While the ribs cook, make the glaze. Remove the dried chiles from the soaking liquid and discard the stem and seeds. Place the chiles in a blender along with the tamarind paste, brown sugar, Worcestershire sauce, lemon and orange juices, and garlic. Purée to make a thick paste, scraping the jar as necessary. Add some of the chile soaking liquid if it seems too thick. Set aside one-fourth of the glaze for serving.

4 After the ribs have cooked for 30 minutes at 400°F., begin basting them with the glaze every 15 minutes until the ribs are tender, about 1 more hour, turning the ribs meaty side up again after 30 minutes. Remove the ribs from the oven, use a clean basting brush to brush them with the reserved glaze, and serve.

mexican pulled pork (tinga poblana)

SERVES 8

1 pound (about 3 medium) russet potatoes, peeled and diced

1 2- to 3-pound pork loin

1 yellow onion, chopped, plus ½ yellow onion left whole

2 garlic cloves, smashed

2 bay leaves

12 ounces raw chorizo, casing removed

5 small tomatoes, peeled, cored, and chopped

2 canned chipotle chiles en adobo, finely chopped (seeded and ribbed for less heat)

2 tablespoons apple cider vinegar

1 teaspoon dried thyme

½ teaspoon dried marjoram

Salt

FOR SERVING

16 corn or flour tortillas

4 medium Hass avocados, halved, pitted, peeled, and sliced

1 cup fresh cilantro leaves

Lime wedges

Tinga Poblana is a sensual, eat-with-your-hands experience, a traditional shredded pork dish from the Puebla state of Mexico that is eaten in a warm flour tortilla with some avocado, fresh cilantro, and a squeeze of lime. I love to serve this kind of food to my friends, especially those who frequently eat in restaurants. This is soul food, the kind of hearty meal where nothing is left on a plate and where you end the night leaning back in a chair, shoes under the table, laughing, drinking, and having a great, relaxed time. People who don't cook especially appreciate this kind of homey dish. Making a simple one-dish meal instead of something fancy with lots of components and sauces also takes a lot of pressure off of the cook. Add a salad, a loaf of bread, and some wine or *cerveza* (that's beer!) and you have a party. Though potato is traditional in this dish, I don't consider it essential and I sometimes leave it out. Add it or not, it's your call. I like to use pork loin instead of fattier cuts like pork shoulder, since it makes for a cleaner-tasting dish.

1 Bring a large pot of salted water to a boil. Add the potatoes and cook until tender, about 20 minutes. Drain the potatoes and set aside.

2 Place the pork in a large pot of water. Add the onion half, the garlic, and the bay leaves and bring to a boil. Reduce the heat to low and simmer gently until the pork is cooked through, about 45 minutes (you can cut off a small chunk and see if it is still pink in the middle). Remove the pork from the water and set it aside until it is cool enough to handle (discard the cooking liquid). Using your fingers or two forks, shred the meat into small pieces and set aside.

(recipe continues)

3 Break the chorizo into small pieces and fry it over medium-high heat in a large skillet or pot, stirring often, until it is completely cooked through, 8 to 10 minutes. Use a slotted spoon to transfer the chorizo to a paper-towel-lined plate. Add the chopped onion to the same skillet and cook, stirring occasionally, until soft, 3 to 5 minutes. Add the shredded pork, the potatoes, the tomatoes, and the chipotle chiles and cook until the tomatoes break down and release their juices, about 15 minutes. Return the cooked chorizo to the pan and stir in the vinegar, thyme, marjoram, and some salt. Continue to cook over medium heat until some of the liquid has evaporated, about 5 minutes.

4 While the pork cooks, heat a medium skillet over medium-high heat. Add a tortilla and warm for 10 to 15 seconds. Flip the tortilla over and continue to warm until the tortilla is pliable and heated through, another 10 to 20 seconds. Place on a plate, cover with a kitchen towel, and set aside; repeat with the remaining tortillas. (Or warm the tortillas in the microwave: Stack them on a plate and cover with a damp cloth, microwave for 30 seconds, and keep them covered until you're ready to serve.)

5 Place the tinga in a serving bowl or bring it to the table in the cooking pot. Arrange the tortillas, avocados, and cilantro on a platter so each diner can fill a tortilla with some of the meat and accompaniments. Pass a bowl of lime wedges around the table to squeeze over each serving.

chile lamb tenders with tomatoes

SERVES 4

1 pound lamb loin, trimmed of fat and silver skin and cut into thin strips

Salt and freshly ground pepper

2 tablespoons olive oil

2 garlic cloves, smashed

1 teaspoon red pepper flakes

12 cherry tomatoes, halved

1 cup baby spinach leaves

Lemon wedges, for serving

Tender and flavorful, lamb loin cut into strips also cooks quickly. The garlicky tomato sauce takes just 3 minutes to cook; triple the quantity and serve it over a piece of seared salmon or tossed with some penne pasta. It's very fresh-tasting; you really don't lose any of the cherry tomatoes' spunk. You can try the recipe with chicken tenders, flank steak cut into strips, or a pork loin cut into strips.

1 Season the lamb strips with some salt and pepper. Heat the oil in a large skillet over high heat. Add the lamb and sear until browned on all sides, 7 to 8 minutes. Transfer the lamb to a plate and set aside.

2 Add the garlic, red pepper flakes, and cherry tomatoes to the same skillet and cook until the tomatoes are soft, 2 to 3 minutes. Remove the garlic from the skillet and discard. Season the sauce with salt and pepper to taste. Return the lamb to the skillet and add the spinach leaves, tossing to combine. Serve with the lemon wedges.

lamb chops with cilantro-mint chimichurri

SERVES 4 TO 6

FOR THE CHIMICHURRI SAUCE

1 packed cup fresh cilantro leaves

½ cup fresh flat-leaf parsley leaves

2 tablespoons fresh mint leaves

1 to 2 pickled or fresh serrano chiles, halved (seeded and ribbed for less heat)

3 tablespoons rice vinegar

1 tablespoon fresh lime juice (from about ½ lime)

1 tablespoon honey

½ teaspoon salt, plus extra for seasoning the lamb

2 tablespoons olive oil

FOR THE LAMB

12 1-inch-thick lamb loin chops, trimmed of excess fat

Salt and freshly ground pepper

2 tablespoons olive oil

3 tablespoons chopped fresh rosemary

3 garlic cloves, peeled and coarsely chopped

Argentine chimichurri sauce is traditionally served with grilled meats. It tastes so good that many Latin countries followed Argentina's lead, coming up with their own adaptations to serve with meat from the grill. My chimichurri includes mint, a classic lamb accompaniment, as well as honey and serrano chiles for a little sweet-spicy action. This sauce is fantastic with any broiled, pan-seared, or grilled meat and even with roasted vegetables. Because so many fresh herbs are used, it's best eaten within a day of making.

1 To make the chimichurri, combine the cilantro, parsley, mint, serrano chile, rice vinegar, lime juice, honey, and salt in the bowl of a food processor and pulse into a paste. With the food processor running, gradually add the olive oil, continuing to process until the sauce is smooth, scraping down the sides of the food processor as necessary. Transfer the chimichurri to a bowl, cover with plastic wrap, and refrigerate for up to 3 hours. (Bring to room temperature before serving.)

2 To make the lamb, preheat your broiler to high and place the oven rack at its highest position.

3 Season the lamb with salt and pepper. Heat the olive oil in a large oven-safe skillet over high heat. Add the lamb chops and brown on all sides, about 10 minutes total. Add the rosemary and the garlic and cook until fragrant, 1 to 2 minutes. Transfer the skillet to the broiler and cook until the lamb is still pink in the center, about 5 minutes. Serve the chops from the oven with a spoonful of the chimichurri drizzled on top.

chipotle beef noodles

SERVES 4

2 tablespoons unsalted butter

¼ cup all-purpose flour

2 cups homemade or canned low-sodium chicken broth

1 small canned chipotle chile en adobo (or more to taste), seeded and minced, plus 1 teaspoon adobo sauce (optional)

½ teaspoon chile powder (or more if desired)

⅔ pound lean ground beef

1 small yellow onion, finely chopped

1 garlic clove, finely minced

Salt and freshly ground pepper

10 ounces wide egg noodles

2 cups grated Cheddar cheese

1 cup chopped fresh cilantro leaves

If you like Italian Bolognese sauce, this will be right up your alley. You can substitute any kind of meat that you like for the ground beef, including ground veal or pork, sliced chicken tenders, or crumbled chorizo, or combine equal amounts of any two for more depth of flavor.

1 Melt 1 tablespoon of the butter in a medium saucepan over medium heat. Stir in the flour using a wooden spoon. Let the paste cook, stirring constantly, until it is pale blond, about 2 minutes. Gradually stir a little of the chicken broth into the flour mixture. Keep adding the broth a little at a time until you have a smooth paste, then whisk in the remaining broth. Add the chipotle chile, the adobo sauce (if using), and the chile powder; bring to a simmer and then reduce the heat to very low and keep warm until the meat mixture is ready.

2 Bring a large pot of water to a boil for the noodles.

3 Melt the remaining tablespoon of butter in a large skillet over medium-high heat. Add the ground beef, onion, garlic, and some salt and pepper. Cook the meat, breaking it up with a wooden spoon as it cooks, until the meat is browned, 5 to 8 minutes. Pour off some of the fat in the skillet (place a too-small pot cover in the skillet and use it to hold the meat mixture), then add the sauce to the meat and stir together.

4 When the water boils, add a large pinch of salt and the noodles. Cook according to the package instructions or until they are al dente. Drain the noodles and stir into the meat sauce. Serve in bowls, sprinkled with the cheese and cilantro.

mini cuban "fritas" (burgers)

SERVES 6

1½ cups dried bread crumbs

¼ cup whole milk

2 pounds lean ground beef

1 large yellow onion, grated on the large-hole side of a box grater

1 large egg, lightly beaten

2 tablespoons fresh lime juice (from about 1 lime)

3 tablespoons ketchup, plus extra for serving

3 garlic cloves, finely minced

1 tablespoon salt

¾ teaspoon paprika

Freshly ground pepper

1 tablespoon olive oil

12 mini hamburger rolls or Cuban rolls

Shoestring potato sticks or chips, for serving

El Rey de las Fritas ("King of the Fried Burgers") is a legendary Miami hole-in-the-wall restaurant where they serve the most amazing burgers. Their secret? The burgers are fried! Because a burger is already pretty decadent, I oven-bake mine instead. I also make them in a mini size; they're cute for parties, or serve two per person with a buffet of all kinds of toppings for a fun dinner party. If you don't want to make minis, just make the patties bigger.

1 Place the bread crumbs in a large bowl. Cover with the milk and soak for 2 minutes. Add the ground beef, onion, beaten egg, lime juice, ketchup, garlic, salt, paprika, and a pinch of pepper and work the ingredients together with your hands or a wooden spoon just until combined. Form the mixture into 12 small 1-inch-thick patties and refrigerate them for at least 45 minutes or up to 8 hours.

2 Heat the olive oil in a large skillet over medium-high heat. Add about half of the burgers and brown them on each side, 5 to 7 minutes total. Keep warm while you cook the remaining burgers.

3 Set the fritas on the rolls. Top each burger with generous amounts of ketchup and shoestring French fries or potato chips, then add the bun tops and serve.

chica tip: For the freshest ground beef, ask your butcher to grind it for you on the spot. Pick out the steak you want (such as a boneless sirloin steak) and give the butcher a nice smile. They'll usually go the extra mile for you. It also helps if you shop for groceries during off-peak times.

latin lasagna (pastelón)

SERVES 6

4 tablespoons (½ stick) unsalted butter, plus 1 tablespoon at room temperature

1 medium yellow onion, finely chopped

¼ cup all-purpose flour

1 teaspoon ground cumin

1¾ cups homemade or canned low-sodium chicken broth

1 cup milk

2½ cups shredded pepper Jack cheese

6 ounces raw chorizo, casings removed

1 pound ground white or dark meat turkey

2 tablespoons Worcestershire sauce (or 1 tablespoon Worcestershire sauce and 1 tablespoon sherry)

1 tablespoon fresh lemon juice (from ½ lemon)

1 teaspoon dried oregano

½ teaspoon salt

Freshly ground pepper

4 very ripe black-skinned plantains, peeled and thinly sliced lengthwise

Paprika

Chopped fresh cilantro leaves, for serving

This is the kind of dish you make when you just want to chow down. Every culture has its own layered casserole. Here, long strips of ripe plantain separate the layers. This dish is sweet, savory, fulfilling, and comforting, with the leanness of the turkey and the spice of the chorizo playing off of the soft and buttery plantains.

1 Preheat your oven to 350°F. Grease a 9 x 13-inch lasagna pan with the tablespoon of softened butter and set it aside.

2 Melt the remaining 4 tablespoons of butter in a medium saucepan over medium heat. Add the onion and cook until it is soft, about 5 minutes. Stir in the flour and cumin and cook for 1 minute before gradually stirring in the chicken broth. Once all of the broth is added, stir in the milk. Continue to stir constantly until the sauce thickens slightly, 8 to 10 minutes. Add 2 cups of the grated cheese and stir the sauce until the cheese has melted. Turn off the heat and transfer the sauce to a medium bowl. Place a piece of plastic wrap directly on the sauce to prevent a skin from forming.

3 Heat a large skillet over medium-high heat and add the chorizo. Cook, using a wooden spoon to break up any large pieces, until it starts to brown, about 4 minutes. Add the turkey and continue to cook until both meats are browned, 8 to 10 minutes. Stir in the Worcestershire sauce, lemon juice, oregano, salt, and some pepper. Remove the skillet from the heat and drain off any excess oil.

4 Line the pan with about one-third of the plantain slices, making sure that they don't overlap. Top the plantains with half of the meat mixture, spreading it out into an even layer so it covers the plantains. Top with half of the cheese sauce. Add another single layer of plantain slices and cover with the remaining meat mixture and the remaining sauce. Top with the rest of the plantains and sprinkle with the remaining cheese and some paprika over the top. Bake until the sauce is bubbly, 45 to 60 minutes. Let the lasagna cool for 10 minutes, sprinkle with the cilantro, and serve.

stir-fried flank steak with tomato-onion jam (peruvian beef saltado)

SERVES 4

1 tablespoon canola or vegetable oil

1 to 1½ pounds flank steak, sliced into 1½-inch wide strips

1 large red onion, quartered and thinly sliced

1 large tomato, cored, halved, and sliced

1 garlic clove, finely minced

Salt and freshly ground pepper

2 teaspoons soy sauce

1 teaspoon red wine vinegar

When I eat beef saltado, a Latin-style steak stir-fry, I feel like I'm home. To me, this is as real as food gets. It's rustic, fast, and comfy and can be easily increased or decreased to serve a bunch of people or just yourself. It's really tasty with a big plate of french fries.

1 Heat the oil in a large wok or skillet over medium-high heat. Add the steak and stir-fry, cooking until it is browned on all sides, 8 to 10 minutes. Transfer the steak to a plate and set it aside.

2 Add the onion, tomato, garlic, and salt and pepper to the same skillet and cook until the onion is soft and the tomato starts to break down, 2 to 4 minutes. Return the beef to the skillet and add the soy sauce and vinegar. Cook for 1 minute, season with salt and pepper to taste, and serve.

cilantro-crusted roast beef

SERVES 6

1 4-pound boneless rump roast, trimmed of fat

6 garlic cloves, coarsely chopped

1 teaspoon celery seed

2 teaspoons coarse salt, plus more to taste

1 teaspoon freshly ground pepper, plus more to taste

2 cups finely chopped fresh cilantro leaves

4 medium sweet potatoes (about 1½ pounds), scrubbed, halved, and quartered

12 large shallots, peeled and halved lengthwise

2 tablespoons olive oil

The smell of a roast in the oven is aromatherapy to my stomach. You can roast just about any vegetable under the meat, such as fennel (one of my favorites), red onions, potatoes, parsnips, or carrots.

1 Set the roast on an aluminum-foil-lined broiler pan and let it sit at room temperature for 1 hour. Preheat your oven to 325°F.

2 Pulse the garlic, celery seed, salt, and pepper in a food processor until it reaches a pasty consistency. Rub it all over the roast and then pat the cilantro onto the roast.

3 Place the sweet potatoes and shallots in a large bowl, toss with the olive oil and some salt and pepper, and set aside.

4 Brush the cilantro off of the meat and discard; cook the roast for 30 minutes. Add the vegetables to the broiler pan and roast for about 1 hour for a rare roast (its internal temperature will read 125°F. on a digital thermometer), or for 1 hour and 10 to 20 minutes for a medium-rare or medium roast, stirring the vegetables every 20 to 30 minutes. Remove the meat and vegetables from the oven and let the meat rest for 10 minutes before slicing. Serve with the pan drippings and the sweet potatoes and shallots on the side.

two-way argentinean barbecued steak (churrasco)

SERVES 4 TO 6

FOR THE CHIMICHURRI

½ cup red wine vinegar

2 tablespoons fresh lemon juice (from ½ lemon)

¾ cup chopped fresh flat-leaf parsley leaves

3 tablespoons chopped fresh oregano leaves

2 garlic cloves, coarsely chopped

2 tablespoons olive oil

⅛ teaspoon red pepper flakes (or more to taste)

FOR THE PINEAPPLE AÏOLI

¾ cup mayonnaise

4 garlic cloves, finely minced

¼ cup canned crushed pineapple in juice, drained

¼ teaspoon grated lime zest

Salt and freshly ground pepper

FOR THE STEAK

2 pounds skirt steak

3 tablespoons olive oil

Salt

The skirt steak, which in Latin America is called *churrasco,* is my favorite cut of meat; I'll order it over a filet mignon anytime. It has a great tender-toothy texture whether pan-fried, broiled, or grilled. It's also pretty cheap, and it is the cut I always turn to when I want to serve meat to a lot of people. The two sauces—a traditional chimichurri and a mock pineapple aïoli— make for an especially festive spread, but they are both delicious, so if you decide to make just one no one will complain!

1 To make the chimichurri, place the vinegar, lemon juice, parsley, oregano, and garlic in a blender and purée. With the motor running, add the olive oil, blending until the sauce comes together. Add the red pepper flakes. Transfer the chimichurri to an airtight container and refrigerate for up to 1 day. Serve at room temperature.

2 To make the pineapple aïoli, mix the ingredients together in a medium bowl. Cover with plastic wrap, refrigerate until thoroughly chilled, and serve within a couple of hours.

3 To make the steak, preheat your grill to high or preheat a ridged grill pan until very hot. Rub the steaks with the olive oil and season them with salt. Grill the steaks for 3 to 4 minutes on each side for a medium-rare to medium steak, or longer for medium well or well done. Serve with any or all of the suggested sauces.

coffee-rubbed filets with sage–blue cheese butter

SERVES 4

2 tablespoons finely ground coffee

1 tablespoon plus 1½ teaspoons freshly ground black pepper

4 6-ounce filets mignons

2 tablespoons canola or vegetable oil

5½ tablespoons unsalted butter, at room temperature

2 teaspoons chopped fresh sage

2 to 3 ounces blue cheese, crumbled

Salt

2 tablespoons dark rum

chica tip: Flavored butters are a great convenience food. You can add just about any herb or spice you can think up, such as ginger, garlic, rosemary, cumin, and even citrus zest. Roll the flavored butter into a log, wrap in plastic wrap, and refrigerate for up to a week or freeze. Top a steak, a chicken breast, or cooked vegetables with a chunk for an instant pop of fresh flavor.

Latin America has been cultivating coffee plants since the eighteenth century and is known to harvest some of the world's finest, most robust coffee beans, the foundation for this amazing smoky and slightly bitter rub. It really accentuates the juicy and almost sweet qualities of a tender filet mignon.

1 Mix the ground coffee and black pepper together in a small bowl. Place the steaks in a baking dish and evenly coat them with the 2 tablespoons of oil. Rub both sides of the steaks with the coffee mixture, cover the baking dish with plastic wrap, and set aside.

2 Mix 4 tablespoons of the softened butter with the sage and blue cheese in a small bowl until well blended. Transfer the butter mixture onto a sheet of plastic wrap and fold the plastic wrap around the butter, shaping the butter into a log. Freeze until the butter is firm and then slice the log into 4 rounds. Keep the rounds in your fridge until the steaks are done.

3 Heat the remaining 1½ tablespoons of butter in a large skillet over high heat. Remove the steaks from the marinade, pat dry with paper towels, sprinkle with salt, and cook until browned on one side, 2 to 4 minutes. Turn the steaks, sprinkle with more salt, and cook on the other side for 1 minute. Reduce the heat to medium low and cook for an additional 3 to 4 minutes for medium-rare or longer if you prefer your steak well done. Transfer the steaks to serving plates and top with a slice of the flavored butter. Add the rum to the skillet and carefully light it with a long match to burn off the alcohol (the flames will go out after a few seconds). Spoon some of the sauce over the steaks and serve immediately.

shredded steak with peppers, onions, and tomatoes (ropa vieja)

SERVES 4

1½- to 2-pound flank steak

3 tablespoons Delicioso Adobo Seasoning (page 22) or purchased adobo (see "The Delicioso Pantry," page 10)

2 tablespoons Worcestershire sauce

2 cups beer

2 tablespoons canola or vegetable oil

¼ red bell pepper, cored, seeded, ribbed, and chopped

¼ green bell pepper, cored, seeded, ribbed, and chopped

1 medium yellow onion, chopped

4 scallions, white and light green parts only, chopped

1 small tomato, cored, halved, and chopped

Salt and freshly ground pepper

Most of the world knows ropa vieja as a Cuban dish, but many Latin American countries make similar versions, and I grew up eating it at least once a week. It's made from flank steak that is cooked for a long, long time, until it is fall-apart tender. Quickly sautéed peppers and onions create this amazing crisp-tender contrast between the slow-cooked meat and the fast-cooked veggies. I use beer in my recipe; it adds an herbiness that I really like, and it tenderizes the meat even more. My favorite way to eat ropa vieja is with ripe plantains. I bake them at 400°F. to accentuate their sweetness.

If you want ropa vieja really fast, shorten the cooking process by microwaving the steak with the marinade for 15 minutes. Turn the beef over and cook until it is tender, about another 15 minutes, and then proceed with the recipe as instructed below.

1 Cut the flank steak into 3 large pieces and place them in a large bowl. In a small bowl, combine the adobo and the Worcestershire sauce. Rub the paste into the steaks, add the beer, and let the steaks marinate for 15 minutes. Transfer the meat and the marinade to a large nonreactive pot and bring it to a boil. Reduce the heat to low, cover, and simmer until the meat is tender, 1 to 1½ hours.

2 Remove the meat from the pot and reserve the cooking liquid. Using two forks, shred the beef and set it aside. Heat the oil in a large skillet over medium-high heat. Add the bell peppers, onion, scallions, and tomato and cook until they are soft, 5 to 8 minutes. Add the beef to the skillet along with ¼ cup of the reserved cooking liquid and some salt and pepper and simmer until the juices have almost evaporated, about 10 minutes. Serve with fried ripe plantains or rice.

my favorite rice and bean recipes

If I had to choose what my last meal on Earth would be, you can bet that rice and beans would be a part of it. In most of Latin America, rice and beans are a part of practically every meal, even breakfast sometimes. With a bowl of rice and beans, I am content and the world is a good place.

If I have the time, I make my beans from scratch, soaking the dry beans overnight with some baking soda (it helps make the beans more digestible) before cooking them for a couple of hours the next day. The texture of fresh-cooked beans is really special, and the bean broth you end up with in the pot is the secret "how-can-it-be-so-good?" ingredient to many grandmother-style recipes. However, I am no saint and I must confess that, yes, I do have a pantry full of canned beans: black beans, pinto beans, chickpeas, white beans. Nothing beats a can of beans for a quick and healthy dinner. Add some cooked veggies and herbs, and that's that.

When it comes to rice, you can bet that I am particular. I like mine moist and very cooked; the method on page 185 is the same one that my mother learned from her mother, who probably learned it from her mother before that. To me, this is the best rice: tender, comforting, not dry. While I most often eat my white rice plainly and simply, sometimes I flavor it with ingredients such as cilantro, tomatoes, coconut, and even Coca-Cola. Try the flavored rice dishes; I think you'll be pleased by your discoveries.

I just can't imagine my life without these two staples. Rice and beans make me happy, and because happiness leads to longer lives, I conclude that eating more rice and beans, not less, is the solution! Life is too short to deprive ourselves of happiness, so go ahead, take a big helping of rice and beans, and live a long life full of joy.

easy gaucho beans

SERVES 6

1 pound dried red kidney
beans, picked over and
rinsed, or 2 15-ounce cans
red kidney beans, rinsed
and drained

1 teaspoon baking soda

4 raw bacon strips,
chopped

1 tablespoon vegetable oil

1 large yellow onion, finely
chopped

8 scallions, white and light
green parts only, finely
chopped

4 medium tomatoes,
peeled, cored, and
chopped

3 large carrots, grated

1 garlic clove, finely minced

1 bay leaf

½ teaspoon Worcestershire
sauce

½ teaspoon ground cumin

½ teaspoon salt

Antioquia in northwest Colombia is one of the most beautiful places on Earth. Just imagine: mountainous and fertile, offering sunny blue-sky days with temperatures in the seventies and crisp sweater-weather nights. It's also cowboy country, and the food, like these saucy beans, is hearty and homey. Add some rice, fried eggs, and steak and you have a meal fit for the most rugged gaucho. If you don't feel like chopping the vegetables, just pulse the onion, scallions, carrots, and garlic in your food processor until they're finely chopped, then add the tomatoes and pulse two or three times until chopped.

1 If using dried beans, soak them in cold water overnight with ½ teaspoon of baking soda. The following day, drain the beans and place them in a large pot with the bacon, another ½ teaspoon of baking soda, and 6 cups of water. Bring to a boil, reduce the heat to a simmer, and cook the beans until they are soft and tender, about 2 hours. If the water level gets low before the beans are tender, add another cup of water (or more as needed). If using canned beans, warm them in a large pot with 3½ cups of water.

2 Heat the oil in a large skillet over medium-high heat for 1 minute. Add the remaining ingredients and cook, stirring often, until the vegetables are soft and fragrant, 5 to 7 minutes.

3 Add the vegetable mixture to the pot with the beans and cook just long enough to bring the flavors together, about 10 minutes. Remove the bay leaf before serving.

chica tip: If using canned beans, simply add the bacon and veggies after they have been sautéed.

frijoles rancheros
(the long and the short)

SERVES 4 TO 6

1 cup dried pinto beans, picked over and rinsed, or 3 cups canned pinto beans, rinsed and drained

2 bay leaves

1 teaspoon dried oregano

½ pound sliced bacon, cut crosswise into ½-inch pieces

1 medium yellow onion, finely chopped

2 teaspoons ground cumin

1 14-ounce can chopped tomatoes, drained (if you're using canned beans, save the tomato liquid)

2 jalapeños, one stemmed, seeded, ribbed, and chopped, the other sliced in rounds for serving

½ teaspoon salt

⅛ teaspoon freshly ground pepper

Sometimes, and I wish it were more often, I am a good girl and cook my beans from scratch. But most times, I opt for the easy way out and use canned beans. For this recipe, you choose: slow cooked and traditional, or quick and easy. Each method has its advantages, though I'll leave it up to you to decide which is better.

1 If using dried beans, soak them overnight in cold water. The following day, drain the beans and place them in a large saucepan with enough water to cover them by 1 inch. Add the bay leaves and oregano and bring to a boil. Reduce the heat to medium low and simmer until the beans are nearly tender, about 1½ hours, adding more water as needed.

2 Meanwhile, heat a large skillet over high heat for 2 minutes. Add the bacon and fry, stirring frequently, until it is crispy, about 6 minutes. Transfer the bacon to a paper-towel-lined plate to drain (discard all but 1 tablespoon of bacon fat in the skillet and set the skillet aside to use later for frying the onion) and then add the bacon to the beans in the pot. Continue cooking the beans, stirring occasionally, until they're tender, 45 minutes to 1 hour. If the pan looks dry, add more water.

3 Heat the reserved bacon fat over medium-high heat for 1 minute. Add the onion and cumin and cook, stirring often, until the onion is softened, about 2 minutes. Add the tomatoes, chopped jalapeño, salt, and pepper and cook until the jalapeño is tender, about 3 minutes. Stir the tomato and onion mixture into the beans and simmer until the flavors come together, about 10 minutes. Discard the bay leaves. Serve hot in bowls with a couple of sliced jalapeños on top.

(recipe continues)

shortcut rancheros

1 Fry the bacon as instructed on page 178 and transfer it to a paper-towel-lined plate (discard all but 1 tablespoon of the bacon fat in the skillet and set the skillet aside to use later for frying the onion).

2 Heat the bacon fat over medium-high heat for 1 minute. Add the onion and cumin and cook, stirring often, until the onion is soft, about 2 minutes. Add the canned beans, bay leaves, oregano, tomatoes and the tomato juice, chopped jalapeño, reserved bacon, salt, and pepper and cook until the flavors come together, 10 to 15 minutes. Serve hot in bowls with a couple of sliced jalapeños on top.

best chica tip ever:
If you decide to make beans from scratch, soak them with ½ teaspoon baking soda, and when cooking them, add another ½ teaspoon baking soda. This will neutralize the complex sugars that cause indigestion and other side effects!

dad's black beans

SERVES 4

1 tablespoon olive oil

1 small yellow onion, finely minced

2 garlic cloves, finely minced

1 bay leaf

½ teaspoon sweet paprika

½ teaspoon salt

2 15-ounce cans black beans, rinsed and drained

½ teaspoon Tabasco

¼ cup dry sherry

This is my dad's recipe for the best black beans I have ever had—and believe me, I've had many!

1 Heat the oil in a medium saucepan over medium-high heat for 1 minute. Add the onion, garlic, and bay leaf and cook, stirring often, until the onion is soft, about 2 minutes.

2 Stir in the paprika and salt and cook for 30 seconds, or until the paprika is fragrant. Add the beans and cook, stirring often, until heated through, about 5 minutes. Add the Tabasco and sherry, bring to a simmer, and cook for 1 minute. Serve immediately or allow to cool, transfer to a resealable freezer bag, and freeze for up to 1 month.

chickpeas in a flash

SERVES 4

1 pound (2 cups) canned chickpeas, rinsed and drained

1 medium red, white, or yellow onion, finely chopped

½ green bell pepper, cored, seeded, ribbed, and finely chopped

1 medium tomato, cored, halved, seeded, and finely chopped

2 tablespoons chopped fresh flat-leaf parsley leaves

⅓ cup olive oil

⅓ cup lemon juice (from about 1½ lemons)

Salt and freshly ground pepper

1 hard-boiled egg, peeled and chopped

This chickpea recipe works for just about any occasion you can think of. It's excellent for breakfast with fried eggs; for a party or cocktails as part of a mezze platter; for picnic fare; and as an easy lunch on the go. I usually have all of these ingredients lying around, so when I'm at a loss for what to make for lunch or dinner, this is what I whip up. With a grilled chicken breast or a pan-seared piece of fish, I'm totally happy.

1 Place the chickpeas in a medium bowl and toss with the onion, bell pepper, tomato, and parsley.

2 Whisk the olive oil and lemon juice together in a separate bowl, then add to the chickpeas and stir to coat all the ingredients. Season to taste with salt and pepper, add the eggs, toss gently, and serve.

last-minute lentils

SERVES 4

1½ cups dried brown lentils, rinsed and drained

1 medium shallot, halved and finely chopped

1 heaping tablespoon Dijon mustard

1 teaspoon sherry vinegar

Salt and freshly ground pepper

Extra-virgin olive oil, for serving (optional)

These are delicious warm, at room temperature, or cold, and they serve as a great sidekick to salmon, cod, a chicken breast, or a pork chop. Keep these ingredients in your pantry so you can have a healthy meal ready in thirty minutes. If you're pressed for time, use one 15-ounce can of lentils, rinsed and drained under cold water, instead of making the lentils from scratch.

1 Place the lentils in a large saucepan with 3 cups of water. Bring to a boil, cover, and reduce the heat to medium low. Simmer for 25 to 30 minutes, or until the lentils are tender. Remove from the heat.

2 In a large bowl, whisk the shallot, mustard, and vinegar together. Add the lentils and some salt and pepper and toss to combine. Serve chilled or at room temperature, drizzled with a little olive oil if you like.

best basic white rice

SERVES 4 TO 6

2 cups long-grain white rice

4 cups homemade or canned low-sodium chicken broth (or water)

1 tablespoon unsalted butter

1½ teaspoons olive oil

1 teaspoon salt

It's often the simplest foods that we're the pickiest about: the perfect scrambled egg, the fluffiness factor of a pancake, the eternal debate over crisp versus chewy chocolate chip cookies (crisp!). Making great white rice is no exception to this rule, and I've discovered that everyone has his or her own preferred way of cooking it. I like mine sort of wet, with popped, open grains. If you agree with my preference, then you will never go wrong making this rice recipe. For a little extra flavor, make the rice with vegetable or chicken broth.

1 Place the rice in a large saucepan with the chicken broth, butter, olive oil, and salt. Bring to a boil, uncovered, and cook until you see holes forming on the surface that tunnel down into the rice, about 8 minutes.

2 Reduce the heat to the lowest setting and cover the saucepan. Cook for 20 minutes, then fluff and serve.

chica tip: If you have random odds and ends of vegetables, like a half of an onion or pepper or a few scallions, lurking in your fridge, add them to the pot with the rest of the ingredients to help flavor the rice. Just remember to remove the mushy vegetable before serving.

9

vegetables

my favorite way to eat garden-fresh vegetables is simply steamed or blanched with a drizzle of olive oil and some coarse sea salt for crunch and fresh cracked pepper for spice. Not everyone is like me, though, and to get my friends and family to eat more vegetables, I add fresh and lively flavors like lime, cilantro, and other herbs, and lots of spices—even a bit of cheese. A teaspoon of Worcestershire sauce is the secret to the Broccoli a la Brava recipe (page 195); it gives the broccoli a more complex and interesting flavor. Plantain Smash (page 204), which is kind of like a subtly sweet-spicy version of mashed potatoes, is accented by cayenne pepper and pepper Jack cheese. Red cabbage, mangos, lots of lime juice, and fresh cilantro make Mango and Red Cabbage Slaw (page 206) a colorful celebration of sweet and tangy, with a fantastic crunchy-tender contrast between the mangos and the raw cabbage.

To make adding *delicioso* vegetables to my table even easier, I make sure to visit my grocery store's salad bar regularly. This is the best secret to eliminating lots of chopping and slicing of peppers, cabbage, carrots, mushrooms, lettuce, cucumbers, and squash. Why reinvent the wheel when someone else is willing to do all of the prep work for you? And since I can buy the exact quantity that I need, I often spend *less* money on prediced and sliced veggies than when I start from scratch.

When I know I'm going to be cooking at home for a couple of nights in a row, if I'm already chopping an onion or a pepper for a dish, I'll chop an extra one for the next day. If you wrap the chopped veggies in nonporous plastic wrap or in an airtight container, half your work for the next meal is already done.

broccoli a la brava

SERVES 4

5 cups small broccoli florets (from about 1 large head)

2 tablespoons olive oil

3 to 4 garlic cloves, finely minced

¼ teaspoon red pepper flakes

1 teaspoon Worcestershire sauce

1 teaspoon grated lime zest

There are several months of the year when broccoli is the only green vegetable in the market that looks at all decent. Though it's just fine steamed with a squeeze of lemon juice, this zesty preparation doesn't take much longer and adds a lot of brightness to a winter meal. If you like slightly bitter broccolini, you can use it instead of broccoli.

1 Steam the broccoli in a steamer insert set over boiling water, covered, until it is just cooked but still crisp, 3 to 5 minutes. (You can also blanch the broccoli in a large pot of boiling, salted water until it is crisp-tender, 5 to 7 minutes.) Transfer the broccoli to a large bowl and set aside.

2 Heat the olive oil in a small skillet over medium-low heat for 1 minute. Add the garlic and cook until fragrant, about 1 minute. Stir in the red pepper flakes and Worcestershire sauce. Add the broccoli to the skillet and toss together to marry the flavors. Serve sprinkled with the lime zest.

chica tip: If you find a gorgeous bunch of broccoli at the market, use it as a centerpiece for your table. Trim the bottom of the bunch and wrap raffia all the way around the stem like a bouquet. Place the broccoli in a pretty vase with a little water and you have a stunning arrangement.

spicy, smoky cauliflower mash

SERVES 4 TO 6

4 cups cauliflower florets (from about 1 large head)

1 cup grated mozzarella cheese

½ cup milk

3 tablespoons sour cream

1 tablespoon lime juice (from about ½ lime)

1 to 2 teaspoons adobo sauce

Salt and freshly ground pepper

Chopped fresh cilantro, for serving

Mashed cauliflower is a silkier, lighter alternative to mashed potatoes. A little adobo sauce from a can of chipotle chiles en adobo adds a beautiful smoky nuance; but you don't need to add much—a little bit goes a long way. You can add other root vegetables, too, such as parsnips, celery root, or rutabaga, or a combination of all three. A veggie mash is a great way to get kids and even adults to eat their vegetables. It's also wonderful with chives instead of cilantro and ⅛ teaspoon of grated nutmeg instead of the adobo sauce.

1 Steam the cauliflower in a steamer insert set over boiling water, covered, until it is very soft, 15 to 20 minutes.

2 Transfer the steamed cauliflower to a blender and purée with the cheese, milk, sour cream, and lime juice until smooth, scraping down the sides of the blender jar as necessary. Add the adobo sauce and salt and pepper to taste, pulse a couple more times, and transfer to a serving bowl. Sprinkle with cilantro and serve.

corn pudding

SERVES 6 TO 8

FOR THE CREAMED CORN

Kernels from 6 ears of corn, sliced off of the cob (about 4 cups corn kernels)

¾ cup milk

2 tablespoons butter

Salt and freshly ground pepper

¼ cup heavy cream

1 stick (½ cup) unsalted butter, melted, plus 1 tablespoon at room temperature

4 large eggs, lightly beaten

1 cup yellow cornmeal

1 teaspoon salt

2 cups (1 pint) sour cream

8 ounces Cheddar cheese, grated (about 2 cups)

I could eat this corn pudding every day and never get tired of it. It's creamy, sweet, and comforting, and somehow it tastes even better for breakfast than for dinner! It's extra special with homemade creamed corn, but I'll come clean and admit that I've made it with two 15-ounce cans of creamed corn and it tastes almost as yummy! To take this shortcut, cut the corn, milk, heavy cream, and 2 tablespoons of butter from the recipe. Corn is indigenous to Central and South America. Evidence of the most ancient wild corn on record was found in Mexico City and is believed to be more than 70,000 years old.

1 To make the creamed corn, place ¾ cup of the corn kernels and ½ cup of the milk in a blender and pulse until coarsely puréed.

2 Melt the butter in a large skillet over medium-high heat. Add the remaining 3¼ cups of corn kernels along with any accumulated corn juices, season with salt and pepper, and cook until tender, 2 to 3 minutes. Add the corn purée, the remaining ¼ cup of milk, and the heavy cream and bring to a gentle simmer. Reduce the heat to medium low and cook until the liquid is slightly thickened, 2 to 3 minutes.

3 Preheat your oven to 350°F. Grease an 8 x 11-inch baking dish with the tablespoon of softened butter and set aside.

4 Combine the melted butter, eggs, cornmeal, salt, sour cream, and cheese together in a large bowl. Stir in the creamed corn and blend well. Transfer the mixture to the prepared baking dish and bake until the edges are set but the center still jiggles slightly and a cake tester comes out with just a little moistness, about 1 hour. Cool for 10 minutes before serving.

picante corn with chimichurri butter

SERVES 6

1 tablespoon sherry vinegar

1½ teaspoons fresh lemon juice

⅓ rounded cup chopped fresh flat-leaf parsley leaves

1½ tablespoons chopped fresh oregano leaves

1 garlic clove, coarsely chopped

Red pepper flakes

½ cup (1 stick) unsalted butter, at room temperature

8 ears of corn, husked

Grated cotija cheese, for serving (optional)

Lime wedges, for serving (optional)

Dress up plain boiled or grilled corn with this feisty butter mixture. The chimichurri butter will keep in the fridge for a few days or in the freezer for up to a month. For an even easier side dish, defrost a bag of frozen corn in the microwave and toss with some chimichurri butter before serving. Cotija cheese is a dry, salty, crumbly Mexican cheese. It's fantastic sprinkled on corn. Feta cheese or ricotta salata are good substitutes. Get more servings out of the same quantity of corn by dividing each cob into two or three pieces.

1 Place the vinegar, lemon juice, parsley, oregano, garlic, and red pepper flakes in a food processor and pulse until finely chopped. Transfer the mixture to a piece of cheesecloth or a kitchen towel and wring out the excess liquid. Place the mixture in a small bowl and stir in the butter.

2 Transfer the chimichurri butter to a sheet of plastic wrap and shape it into a log. Wrap in plastic wrap and refrigerate until it has hardened.

3 Meanwhile, bring a large pot of salted water to a boil. Add the corn and boil until it's tender, 5 to 7 minutes. Drain and transfer to a serving platter. Place a disc of chimichurri butter on each ear of corn and serve sprinkled with cotija cheese and with a lime wedge on the side.

green beans with mint and peanuts

SERVES 4

¼ teaspoon salt, plus extra for boiling the green beans

12 ounces green beans, trimmed

½ red bell pepper, cored, seeded, and thinly sliced

⅓ cup extra-virgin olive oil

⅓ cup fresh lime juice (from about 2½ limes)

2 teaspoons sugar

½ cup coarsely chopped dry-roasted, lightly salted peanuts

2 tablespoons chopped fresh cilantro leaves

2 tablespoons chopped fresh mint leaves

If you have tried Indonesian food, you'll recognize the spicy-sweet-tangy flavors in this side dish. It's great with anything grilled, especially fish. For a more East Asian–flavored dish, add some bamboo shoots and freshly grated ginger. As long as your cutting board is out and your knife is already dirty, why not cut the remaining pepper half now and wrap it in plastic wrap for later? You can add the chopped peppers to scrambled eggs, beans, a fish pocket, or a salad.

1 Empty 1 tray of ice cubes into a large bowl of cold water and set aside. Bring a large pot of salted water to a boil and add the green beans. Cook until they're crisp-tender, 6 to 8 minutes. Drain the green beans, then submerge them in the ice water to stop the cooking. Drain the beans and transfer them to a large bowl.

2 Add the bell pepper to the green beans and toss to combine. Whisk the olive oil, lime juice, sugar, and ¼ teaspoon of salt together in a small bowl. Pour the vinaigrette over the beans and peppers. Before serving, sprinkle with the chopped peanuts, cilantro, and mint.

flavor-packed peppers

SERVES 4

1 tablespoon unsalted butter, at room temperature

2 tablespoons olive oil

1 pound lean ground beef

1 medium yellow onion, chopped

1 garlic clove, finely minced

2 small tomatoes, cored, halved, and chopped

1 small green apple, peeled, cored, and chopped

1 tablespoon red wine vinegar

¾ teaspoon Delicioso Seasoning Adobo (page 22) or purchased adobo (see "The Delicioso Pantry," page 10)

3 ounces pitted green olives, coarsely chopped

1 hard-boiled egg, chopped

½ cup chopped fresh flat-leaf parsley leaves

4 large green bell peppers, tops cut off, seeds and ribs removed and bottoms trimmed to make the peppers stand upright

1 cup shredded mozzarella cheese

Paprika

On the outside, these look like your classic stuffed bell peppers. But on the inside—watch out! These stuffed peppers have flavor to spare. Unlike the traditional recipe of rice, ground beef, onions, and maybe some ketchup, mine are packed with loads of aromatics and spices, such as garlic, adobo seasoning, green olives, parsley, and paprika. Mozzarella cheese adds richness, while a green apple hints of sweetness. I love ketchup as much as the next *chica,* but in this recipe I use fresh tomatoes for a light acidy note. These freeze really well, so why not make a double batch? You can pull out a single serving to reheat the next time you're too pooped to cook. For a pretty presentation, stuff one green, orange, red, and yellow bell pepper.

1 Preheat your oven to 350°F. Grease an 8-inch square baking dish with the butter and set aside.

2 Heat the olive oil in a large skillet over medium-high heat. Add the meat and cook, breaking up any large pieces, until it's browned, 5 to 8 minutes. Add the onion and garlic and cook, stirring often, until the onion is soft, about 8 minutes. Stir in the tomatoes, apple, vinegar, and adobo. Reduce the heat to medium low and simmer, covered, until the apple is soft, about 10 minutes. Remove the skillet from the heat and stir in the olives, egg, and parsley.

3 Spoon the mixture into the peppers and top with the cheese. Arrange the stuffed peppers in the prepared baking dish and bake until the peppers are tender and the cheese is melted, 30 to 45 minutes. Sprinkle with a little paprika before serving.

chica tip: Buy a few wide banana leaves (or other nontoxic tropical leaves) in your grocery store's floral department and use them to line plates. They add an exotic and very hip feel to even the most classic, traditional foods.

plantain chips (patacones)

SERVES 4 TO 6

2 green plantains

1 cup vegetable oil, plus more if necessary

Salt

Spicy Scallion-Lime Ají Sauce (page 102)

Also known as tostones, fried plantain chips are savory, crisp, and starchy. If you order them in a restaurant or from a fish shack, they usually come with some fresh green salsa on the side for dipping. Patacones are an unusual and delicious alternative to roasted potatoes with a piece of meat, and they are a fantastic partner to a bowl of beans. They don't reheat very well, so indulge and eat them up while they're hot!

1 Cut off the ends of the plantains and then carefully cut a slit down the length of the skin without cutting into the plantain itself. Using a wooden spoon, pry up the edges of the peel and pull off the skin. Once the peel is removed, cut the plantain crosswise into 3 or 4 pieces, each 2 to 3 inches long.

2 Heat the oil in a medium skillet over high heat until it shimmers, about 3 minutes. Add the plantains and fry them until they turn golden on all sides, about 3 minutes. Use a slotted spoon to transfer them to a paper-towel-lined plate to drain, then place them between 2 sheets of parchment paper. Reduce the heat to medium.

3 Flatten the plantains by pressing down on them with a heavy-bottomed pan. Return half of the flattened plantains to the oil and refry until they are deep golden on both sides, 4 to 6 minutes. Transfer them back to the paper-towel-lined plate to drain and repeat with the remaining flattened plantains. Sprinkle with salt and serve immediately with the ají salsa.

chica tip: The secret to making great tostones is that the oil not be too hot. That way instead of just browning them the first time, you fry them until they are cooked almost all the way through. Then they are flattened and cooked again until crisp.

plantain smash

SERVES 4

4 very ripe black-skinned plantains

5 tablespoons unsalted butter, at room temperature

1 tablespoon finely chopped fresh thyme or 1½ teaspoons dried thyme

Cayenne pepper (optional)

Salt

1½ cups warm whole milk, plus more if necessary

½ cup grated Mexican cheese blend (or ½ cup of pepper Jack or mozzarella)

Sweeter and saltier than mashed potatoes, plantain smash is delicious with any meat dish you can think of. I adore it with slow-roasted pork. You probably could use leftovers for making plantain fritters or dumplings, but I never have leftovers, so you'll have to tell me how they turn out! In Latin markets, plantains are often sold at various intervals of ripeness: green, yellow, and semi-black. Plantains take longer than a banana to ripen, so if you purchase green or yellow plantains, plan on it taking at least 5 days for them to turn completely. You can quicken the ripening by placing them in a paper bag and leaving them out at room temperature.

1 Bring a large pot of water to a boil. Cut the ends off the plantains and boil them until their skin starts to split and a paring knife easily slips into their centers, 15 to 20 minutes; drain. Once the plantains are cool enough to handle, remove the skins and return the plantains to the pot. Mash the plantains, or, for a finer texture, press them through a ricer.

2 Add the butter, thyme, cayenne (if using), and some salt and mix well. Gradually stir in the warm milk, mixing until the plantains reach your desired consistency (I like them medium thick with a few lumps). If they're too thick and sticky for your taste, then drizzle in a little more warm milk. Stir in the cheese, and once it melts, serve immediately.

polenta with tomato–bell pepper sauce

SERVES 4

FOR THE SAUCE

1 tablespoon unsalted butter

½ red bell pepper, cored, seeded, ribbed, and very thinly sliced

½ green bell pepper, cored, seeded, ribbed, and very thinly sliced

1 small yellow onion, very thinly sliced

1 small tomato, cored and chopped

1 tablespoon Maggi seasoning sauce or Worcestershire sauce

Salt and freshly ground pepper

FOR THE POLENTA

2 tablespoons unsalted butter

½ teaspoon salt

1 cup coarsely ground yellow cornmeal

There is a huge population of Italians in Argentina, and Italian dishes like *ñoqui* potato dumplings (gnocchi), pizza, and polenta are ever-popular. This is a Caribbean-style polenta that's eaten throughout the Dutch West Indies and the texture will be slightly softer than that of Italian polenta. It's fantastic with this jammy Creole sauce. Make a double batch of the sauce and use it as a condiment throughout the week; it's fabulous with scrambled or poached eggs, rice, pasta, or roasted chicken.

1 To make the sauce, melt the butter in a medium skillet over medium-high heat. Add the peppers, onion, tomato, Maggi seasoning sauce, and salt and pepper and cook, stirring often, until the peppers and onion are tender and the tomato is jammy, 6 to 8 minutes. Set aside or refrigerate, covered, for up to 3 days.

2 To make the polenta, bring 3 cups of water, the butter, and the salt to a boil in a small saucepan over medium-high heat. Add the cornmeal, reduce the heat to medium low, and continue to cook, stirring constantly, until the mixture thickens and separates from the sides and bottom of the saucepan, about 5 minutes. Cover the polenta with a plate and invert the two dishes so the polenta cake is upside-down. Slide the polenta back onto the original serving dish with the smooth side up. Serve it hot topped with the warmed sauce. (If making the sauce in advance, warm it before serving.)

mango and red cabbage slaw

SERVES 4

1 head of red cabbage, halved and very finely shredded (about 8 cups)

1 teaspoon salt

1 large or 2 small ripe mangos, peeled, fruit cut off of the seed, and diced (see page 50)

1 tablespoon chopped fresh cilantro leaves

¼ cup lime juice (from about 2 limes)

1 tablespoon apple cider vinegar

1 tablespoon granulated sugar

Sweet and tangy, this is a refreshing change to heavy mayonnaise-based coleslaws. It's so good with fried fish chicharrones (page 82) or fried chicken, and it's an absolute must at my barbecues.

1 Place the cabbage in a large bowl and toss it with the salt, using your hands to press down firmly on the cabbage to encourage it to release some of its moisture and better absorb the salt. Transfer the cabbage to a colander set over a bowl or sink and let it sit for 20 minutes to drain.

2 Using paper towels or a kitchen towel, wring as much liquid as possible from the cabbage and place it in a clean, large bowl. Toss with the mangos, cilantro, lime juice, vinegar, and sugar. Let the coleslaw sit at room temperature for 15 minutes before serving.

peruvian potatoes with spicy cream sauce (papas a la huancaina)

SERVES 4

2 medium russet potatoes, scrubbed clean

10 ounces feta cheese, broken into small chunks

⅓ cup evaporated milk

2 to 3 canned ají amarillo chiles, seeded and ribbed (or 3 red or yellow roasted bell peppers, seeded and ribbed, plus 1 tablespoon cayenne pepper)

1 garlic clove, finely minced

½ cup canola or vegetable oil

1 tablespoon lime juice (from about ½ lime)

Salt

4 large lettuce leaves (such as Bibb or romaine)

2 hard-boiled eggs, peeled and sliced, for garnish

2 tablespoons chopped fresh flat-leaf parsley leaves, for garnish

Potatoes are believed to have originated in Peru, and there is evidence suggesting that they were cultivated there some two thousand years ago. There are now about seven hundred varieties on record in every color of the rainbow, from blue and purple to white, yellow, and red. Papas a la Huancaina is often served as a starter in Peru and Bolivia, but it's great as a saucy side dish, too. See "The Delicioso Pantry," page 10, for information about buying ají amarillo chiles.

1 Place the potatoes in a large pot and cover them with water. Bring to a boil and cook for 30 minutes, or until a paring knife slides easily into their centers. Drain the potatoes and let them cool slightly. Peel the potatoes and slice them into ½-inch rounds (you should end up with about 8 slices total). Cover the rounds with plastic wrap and set aside.

2 Place the cheese, evaporated milk, chiles, garlic, oil, and lime juice in a blender and purée. The sauce should be smooth, creamy, and pourable. If the sauce is too thick, add water, 1 tablespoon at a time, until the sauce is thinned out. Season to taste with salt.

3 Place a lettuce leaf on a plate and top with 2 slices of potato. Pour the sauce over the potatoes. Garnish with some hard-boiled egg slices and a sprinkle of parsley.

chica tip: To keep the cheese sauce from forming a skin, place a sheet of plastic wrap directly on its surface before setting aside or refrigerating.

cheesy potatoes (chorreada)

SERVES 4 TO 6

1½ pounds small waxy red, white, or yellow potatoes

1 tablespoon olive oil

4 scallions, white and light green parts only, halved lengthwise and sliced crosswise into 1-inch strips

½ teaspoon tomato paste

2 ripe tomatoes, peeled, cored, and diced

1 teaspoon Delicioso Adobo Seasoning (page 22) or purchased adobo (see "The Delicioso Pantry," page 10)

¼ cup heavy cream

¼ pound grated Edam or Gouda cheese

Salt and freshly ground pepper

Chorreada means "to spill over," and it refers to the generous amount of cheese sauce poured over these potatoes. They're great with steak or chicken; or for a vegetarian meal, just add some plain rice. This dish can also be made with yucca instead of potatoes, which is really easy if you buy bags of frozen yucca. You'll save time peeling the rock-hard tubers, and the flavor is virtually the same.

1 Bring a large pot of salted water to a boil. Add the potatoes and boil until a paring knife easily slips into their center, 15 to 25 minutes, depending on their size.

2 Meanwhile, heat the olive oil in a large skillet over medium-high heat for 1 minute. Add the scallions and cook, stirring often, until they're soft, about 2 minutes. Stir in the tomato paste, cook for 30 seconds, and then add the tomatoes, adobo, and 2 tablespoons of water and cook until the mixture is thickened slightly, about 5 minutes. Stir in the cream, cheese, and some salt and pepper and cook until the cheese has melted.

3 Drain the potatoes and place them in a serving dish. Pour the cheese sauce over the whole potatoes and serve hot.

sweet potato and yuca oven fries

SERVES 6

1 large sweet potato (about 8 ounces), peeled or unpeeled, cut into 4-inch-long and ¼- to ½-inch-thick fries

2 tablespoons olive oil, or more as needed

½ teaspoon chile powder

½ teaspoon ground coriander

Coarse sea salt and freshly ground pepper

8 ounces frozen yuca

Sour cream, for dipping (optional)

Sweet chile sauce, for dipping (optional)

I'm the kind of person who orders a healthy salad at a restaurant and then steals everyone else's fries right off of their plate! I have good intentions, but fried food always wins me over. These oven-baked fries are so flavorful, I never miss the fat. Fresh yuca (cassava) is really difficult to peel, so I don't bother with it and use frozen yuca instead. If you can't find frozen yuca, just use more sweet potatoes.

1 Set one oven rack to the upper-middle position and one to the lower-middle position. Preheat your oven to 450°F. Line 2 baking sheets with aluminum foil and set aside.

2 Place the sweet potato fries in a large bowl and toss with 1 tablespoon of the olive oil, ¼ teaspoon of the chile powder, ¼ teaspoon of the coriander, and some salt and pepper. Transfer the fries to a baking sheet (set the bowl aside for the yuca) and bake on the lower-middle rack until the sweet potato fries start to shrivel, about 20 minutes.

3 Meanwhile, bring a large pot of salted water to a boil. Add the yuca and cook until tender, about 25 minutes, and then drain. Once the yuca is cool enough to handle, cut it into ¼- to ½-inch-thick fries.

4 Place the yuca fries in the reserved large bowl and toss them with the remaining tablespoon of olive oil (add more if needed to coat them), chile powder, coriander, and salt and pepper. Transfer the yuca to the second prepared baking sheet. Move the sweet potatoes to the upper-middle rack and place the yucca on the lower-middle rack. Bake for 10 minutes, and then turn both the sweet potatoes and the yuca over and bake until golden and crisp, 5 to 10 minutes longer. Serve accompanied by a bowl of sour cream and a bowl of sweet chile sauce for dipping, if you like.

feel-good stuffed zucchini

SERVES 4

6 ice cubes

4 medium 6-inch-long zucchini

1 hard-boiled egg, peeled and chopped

¼ cup grated mozzarella cheese

¼ cup half-and-half

½ teaspoon salt

¼ cup dry bread crumbs

¼ cup grated Parmesan cheese

1 teaspoon paprika

1 tablespoon chopped fresh flat-leaf parsley leaves

Wasting food is one of my pet peeves, and I hate needlessly throwing any bit of a vegetable away. When you grow up in a Third World country, you learn quickly to never waste food, as there are so many who go without. For this reason, I don't discard the scooped-out zucchini pulp—not when I can use it in the stuffing for the zucchini. Once you get in this mind-set, you'll find lots of uses for food scraps you might otherwise toss: Add the "heel" of your Parmesan cheese wedge to soup, risotto, or pasta sauce; add leafy celery stalk tops to soup stocks; add leafy beet tops to veggie sautées; and save the fibers and seeds from pumpkins and squash to sauté them in butter or oil for a wonderfully rich base to a squash soup.

1 Preheat your oven to 350°F. Line a rimmed baking sheet with aluminum foil and set aside. Prepare an ice-water bath by placing the ice cubes into a large bowl of cold water.

2 Bring a large pot of water to a boil. Add the zucchini and boil just until softened slightly, 6 to 8 minutes. Drain the zucchini in a colander and plunge them into the ice water to cool. Once the zucchini are cool, remove them from the ice bath, place them on a paper-towel-lined plate, and set aside.

3 Combine the chopped egg, mozzarella, half-and-half, and salt in a small bowl. Cut the zucchini in half lengthwise and use a teaspoon to scrape out the seeds, making a long well. Place the pulp in a fine-mesh sieve and use a spoon to press out the liquid, then mix the pulp into the cheese and egg mixture.

4 Place the hollowed-out zucchini halves on the prepared baking sheet. Fill each one with the cheese and egg mixture. Combine the bread crumbs, Parmesan, and paprika in a small bowl and sprinkle it evenly over the zucchini halves. Bake until the topping is golden brown, 12 to 14 minutes. Serve sprinkled with the chopped parsley.

spicy swiss chard with miso and ginger

SERVES 4 TO 6

FOR THE VINAIGRETTE

1½ tablespoons miso paste

1 tablespoon grated, peeled fresh ginger

½ jalapeño pepper, finely minced (seeded and ribbed for less heat)

2 teaspoons red wine vinegar

1 teaspoon mirin

1 teaspoon soy sauce

2 tablespoons sesame oil

1 medium red onion, halved and thinly sliced

½ teaspoon red pepper flakes

2 pounds Swiss chard, tough stems removed, leafy greens thinly sliced into ribbons

I am a Japanese food addict and have a thing for Asian ingredients like mirin and soy sauce, which add a beautiful refreshing quality to absolutely anything they touch. Mild Swiss chard takes to these flavors like a fish to water. Rainbow chard and red chard can be used interchangeably for Swiss chard, or use a combination of all three for a really colorful dish. Add 2½ tablespoons of sesame oil to the vinaigrette ingredients and you have a fabulous dressing for a raw spinach salad or a broiled fish fillet.

1 To make the vinaigrette, whisk the miso paste, ginger, jalapeño, vinegar, mirin, and soy sauce together in a medium bowl and set aside.

2 Heat the sesame oil in a large skillet over medium-high heat. Add the onion and red pepper flakes and cook, stirring often, until the onion starts to soften, about 3 minutes. Stir in the Swiss chard, then pour in the vinaigrette. Reduce the heat to low, cover, and cook until the Swiss chard is tender, 6 to 8 minutes, and serve.

yuca with cuban mojo

SERVES 4

1 pound frozen yuca

$\frac{2}{3}$ cup lemon juice (from about $2\frac{1}{2}$ lemons)

$\frac{1}{3}$ cup vegetable oil

1 medium yellow onion, thinly sliced

4 to 6 garlic cloves, peeled and thinly sliced

Salt and freshly ground pepper

1 tablespoon chopped fresh oregano leaves

Tía Magda is like a second mother to me; she and my mother have been best friends for more than thirty years. Raised in Cuba, Tía Magda makes the meanest Cuban mojo sauce I've ever tasted. I've never been able to improve on it, which goes to show that some recipes are best left untouched.

1 Bring a large pot of salted water to a boil. Add the yuca and boil until tender, about 30 minutes. Drain the yuca and place it on a serving platter. Sprinkle with the lemon juice.

2 Heat the oil in a small skillet over high heat until it is shimmering, about 3 minutes. Carefully add the onions and garlic, watching for spattering, and cook for $1\frac{1}{2}$ minutes, stirring constantly. Pour the onion, garlic, and oil directly over the yuca. Season the dish to taste with salt and pepper, then sprinkle with the chopped fresh oregano and serve.

bebidas deliciosas:
drink up!

along the beaches, streets, and mountain roads and in the plaza center of nearly every little pueblo you'll see in Latin America, you will find little shacks selling batidos (refreshing smoothies made from water, milk, fruit, and ice). I make them for myself all the time; the best ones always seem to be the craziest ones, made from combinations of whatever fruit I have left over in my fridge.

If I'm in a plan-ahead kind of mood, I'll portion out small quantities of fruit in resealable plastic bags and store them in the fridge or freezer. Then, whenever hunger strikes, the fruit goes into the blender with some milk, water, or ice and just like that, I am fueled and ready for takeoff!

South America and the Caribbean are known for their tropical fruits such as guava, açai berries from the Amazon, papayas, and guanabana (soursop). Tropical juices morph into sophisticated cocktails when blended with alcohol. Even if I'm serving wine with dinner, I like to offer my guests a fun welcome drink that gets everyone in the mood for a great time. Punch is playful yet sophisticated, easy to make, and economical. Since you are blending juice and alcohol, there's no need to use top-shelf alcohol brands, though I do stand by the philosophy that you should cook with (or blend with) wines and alcohols you wouldn't mind drinking straight up.

For a mean fiesta, the way you present your drinks is especially important. Diner-style cocktail shakers with bendy straws or sugar-cane swizzle sticks are fun for batidos and juices. For cocktails and punch, I like to set out an arrangement of stemless glasses: they're less prone to tipping over. Add some cool cocktail napkins and party noshes like plantain chips, stuffed olives, and *canchita* (toasted corn kernels; see page 111) and you're ready to unwind, chat up the *amigos,* and kick up your heels.

tart banana crush

SERVES 4

1-inch piece of fresh ginger, peeled and chopped

¼ cup finely chopped mint leaves

¾ cup lime juice (from about 6 limes)

2 cups fresh orange juice (from about 8 large oranges)

2 bananas, cut into chunks

1 cup ice cubes

Sugar to taste

Lime or orange wedges, for garnish

Avoid blender block-ups by adding the liquid ingredients to the blender first and then adding the chunky ingredients. This will help prevent the solid fruit or ice cream from clogging the blades. To make this into a more substantial breakfast smoothie, add some plain or flavored yogurt.

1 Bring 1 cup of water and the ginger and mint leaves to a boil in a small saucepan. Turn off the heat, cover, and let the ginger and mint leaves steep for 5 minutes. Discard the ginger and mint and let the ginger-mint water cool to room temperature. (The ginger-mint water can be made a day or two ahead and chilled in the fridge.)

2 Combine the lime juice, orange juice, and ginger-mint water in a blender. Turn the blender on and, with the motor running, add the bananas. Once incorporated, add the ice cubes and some sugar and blend until smooth. Serve immediately garnished with a lime or orange wedge.

peachy mint batido

SERVES 4

½ cup fresh mint leaves, plus extra mint sprigs for garnish

3 cups chopped peaches (from about 5 peaches), plus a few extra slices for garnish

1 cup vanilla ice cream

1 cup ice cubes

Peaches and mint make a particularly refreshing combo. I like the texture and richness of ice cream and little bits of peach skin in my batido (plus I am way too lazy to skin peaches), but if you prefer a smooth batido, press the smoothie through a fine-mesh sieve before serving.

1 Bring 1 cup of water and the mint leaves to a boil in a small saucepan. Turn off the heat, cover, and let the mint leaves steep for 5 minutes. Remove the mint leaves and set aside. Let the mint water cool to room temperature.

2 Place the mint leaves and mint water, peaches, ice cream, and ice cubes in a blender and purée until smooth. Serve immediately in chilled glasses and garnish with a slice of peach and a sprig of mint.

chica tip: Make a double batch of mint water and soak washcloths in it; wring them dry and chill them. When guests arrive, give them a minty washcloth to refresh their face, neck, and hands.

guanabana mojitos

SERVES 4

12 fresh mint leaves

2 teaspoons sugar

1 lime, quartered

Ice cubes

2 tablespoons guanabana nectar

½ cup white rum

½ cup club soda

Sugarcane sticks, for serving (optional)

Mojitos are *the* drink in Miami, and I love to experiment with different flavors. If you can't find guanabana nectar, substitute mango, apricot, or—my second favorite mojito add-in— lychee. Smashing the mint with sugar and lime by hand (called muddling) releases the mint's and lime's essential oils. This is what gives the mojito its signature refreshing character.

1 Divide the mint, sugar, and lime wedges among 4 old-fashioned glasses. Using a pestle (from a mortar and pestle) or the end of a wooden spoon, muddle the mint, sugar, and lime together.

2 Add some ice and top off with some nectar, white rum, and club soda. Swirl with a sugarcane stick (if using) and serve.

classic pisco sour

SERVES 4

½ cup Pisco or other brandy

¼ cup lime juice (from about 2 limes)

1 tablespoon simple syrup (see Chica Tip)

1 egg white (optional)

2 dashes Angostura bitters

Ice cubes, for serving

Pisco, a colorless brandy made from grapes, is the most popular spirit consumed in Bolivia, Chile, and Peru. My maternal grandfather was from Bolivia, and I have spent a lot of time there visiting relatives (and drinking many Pisco sours!). The egg white gives the cocktail its signature frothiness, but if you have concerns about raw eggs, you can leave it out.

Place the brandy, lime juice, simple syrup, egg white (if using), and bitters in a blender. Blend until the mixture is frothy. Serve over ice.

chica tip: To make simple syrup, bring ½ cup of water to a simmer in a small saucepan over medium-high heat. Add ½ cup of sugar, stir to dissolve, and turn off the heat. Refrigerate until cold. Simple syrup can keep in your fridge for weeks. Use this liquid sugar in cocktails, iced tea, lemonade, or even whipped cream.

watermelon juice

SERVES 6

½ seedless watermelon (6 to 7 pounds), rind removed, halved, sliced, and cut into 1-inch chunks

16 ice cubes

1 liter chilled lemon-flavored soda

Sugar

Sometimes the best things in life are the most simple. Water-melon, ice, and lemon-flavored soda are all you need to bring you back to life on a hot, humid day. Just looking at a tall glass of hot pink watermelon juice wakes me up! For a festive cock-tail, replace the lemon soda with your favorite sparkling wine.

Place half of the watermelon and 8 ice cubes in a blender and blend until liquefied (once you add the lemon soda it will thin out even more—you can always add more ice cubes if you want it slushier). Slowly add half of the lemon soda and blend until smooth. Pour into glasses; repeat with the remaining watermelon, another 8 ice cubes, and the remaining lemon soda. Add sugar to taste, pour into glasses, and serve.

chica tip: This is the easiest way to cut a whole watermelon: Slice off the rounded top and bottom of the watermelon so it stands upright, then slice away the rind so you are left with a giant watermelon cube. Chop into small chunks or slice. Sprinkle with a little lime juice for a citrusy edge.

guava champagne cocktail

SERVES 4

½ cup guava shells

¼ cup vodka

¼ cup sparkling wine (see Chica Tip)

2 cups lemon sorbet

Fresh mint sprigs, for garnish

Venice, one of my favorite cities in the world, is also home to one of my favorite cocktails, the bubbly Sgroppino. Refreshing and sweet, it's made from Champagne, lemon sorbet, vodka, and mint. I've added guava shells to give my version a gorgeous magenta color. If you can't find guava shells, use canned and drained lychee fruit or fresh mangos instead.

Place the guava shells, vodka, sparkling wine, and lemon sorbet in a blender and purée. Divide among champagne glasses and serve with a mint sprig.

chica tip: Spanish cava, Italian prosecco, and domestic sparkling wine are all delicious and wallet-friendly alternatives to pricey French Champagne.

¼ cup kosher salt

3 tablespoons chile powder

4 limes, quartered

Ice cubes

4 12-ounce bottles of beer

Tabasco sauce

Worcestershire sauce

michelada marías

SERVES 4

Here is the cure for even the worst hangover, and believe me, it works. It's usually made with half soda and half beer, but I like it the Mexican way with beer, limes, and chile powder. In Mexico, it's served with radishes and jicama sticks on the side. It's a fun change-up to Sunday brunch bloody Marys.

1 Combine the salt and chile powder in a small bowl and transfer it to a flat plate. Rub a lime wedge around the rim of each beer mug and dip it into the chile-salt to coat the rim.

2 Squeeze 4 lime wedges into each mug. Add a couple of the juiced wedges to the mug and fill with ice. Add 1 bottle of beer, a dash of Tabasco, and a dash of Worcestershire sauce and serve immediately.

guava-jalapeño margaritas

SERVES 4

3 jalapeños

½ cup plus 2 tablespoons tequila

½ cup plus 2 tablespoons lime juice (from about 5 limes), plus extra lime wedges for the glass rims (optional)

¼ cup Cointreau or Grand Marnier

3 tablespoons guava juice

Coarse salt or margarita salt (optional)

Spicy-sweet, these margaritas really get my juices flowing! To serve this as a frozen margarita, blend the mixture with some ice until it is slushy and use larger margarita glasses instead of martini glasses. Fine or coarse sugar is a yummy change from the traditional salted rim. Note that the tequila and jalapeños need to steep overnight.

1 Place 2 whole jalapeños and the tequila in a small bowl. Cover with plastic wrap and set aside for 1 day.

2 Pour the tequila into a pitcher or a large punch bowl and add the lime juice, Cointreau, and guava juice. Stir to combine and chill in the refrigerator.

3 If you would like to have a salted rim for your margaritas, place the salt on a flat plate. Rub a lime wedge around the rim of each glass, turn it upside down onto the salt, and then twist the glass in the salt to coat the rim.

4 Thinly slice the remaining jalapeño. Serve the margarita straight up in a martini glass with some jalapeños floating in the glass, or slit one side of the jalapeño ring and hang on the side of the glass.

chica tip: Nothing beats a frosty glass on a hot day (or night). Fill each glass with ice water and let it sit for a couple of minutes until the glass is nice and cold. Pour out the ice and water and then place the glasses in your freezer until they get that frosty look. This is a great trick for beer mugs, too.

gigante kiwi mojitos

SERVES 4

1 cup packed fresh mint leaves

2 kiwis, peeled and coarsely chopped

4 tablespoons sugar

Ice cubes

½ cup lime juice (from about 4 limes)

¼ cup white rum

1 liter chilled club soda

Sugarcane sticks, for serving (optional)

Hola, **handsome! Tall, green, and yummy, sweet kiwi makes these mojitos pop. Serve them up in tall glasses with a sugarcane swizzle stick or a fun bendy straw.**

1 Divide the mint leaves, kiwis, and sugar among 4 tall glasses. Using a pestle (from a mortar and pestle) or the end of a wooden spoon, muddle the mint, kiwis, and sugar together.

2 Add some ice and top off with the lime juice, white rum, and club soda. Swirl with a sugarcane stick (if using) or a straw and serve.

tequila sunrise punch

SERVES 4 TO 6

½ cup silver or gold tequila

1 liter chilled citrus-flavored club soda

2 limes, quartered

1 small unpeeled orange, cut into 1-inch chunks

½ small unpeeled grapefruit, cut into 1-inch chunks

Ice cubes

This typical Mexican-style punch is actually pretty close to a Spanish sangria. Not too fruity or girly, this is one punch that the *chicos* **happily line up for. Save your aged Patrón tequila for sipping and use a moderately priced silver or gold tequila.**

1 Pour the tequila and club soda into a pitcher. Add the limes, orange, and grapefruit and set aside for 10 minutes.

2 Add enough ice to the pitcher so that the punch rises to the top. Serve in chilled glasses with some fruit in each glass.

wicked chica punch

SERVES 12 TO 14

2 cups brandy

1 cup sugar

1 pound strawberries, hulled and quartered

1 bottle chilled champagne or sparkling wine

1 bottle chilled light white wine

1 liter chilled club soda or seltzer

I can count on this punch to make any party hop! Watch out, though; it goes down as easily as fruit juice, but if you drink too much, you'll never know what hit you! Let the strawberries soak with the brandy overnight so they're plenty potent. If you don't feel like washing, cleaning, and cutting fresh strawberries, buy frozen instead; they work fine in this recipe.

1 Whisk the brandy and sugar together in a large bowl. Pour into a resealable plastic bag, add the strawberries, and macerate the strawberries in the refrigerator overnight.

2 When you're ready to serve, transfer the strawberries and liquid to a large punch bowl. Add the Champagne, wine, and club soda. Ladle a few macerated strawberries into each glass as you serve.

happy
endings

When it comes to throwing a fabulous and memorable fiesta, ending on a high note is key. I want my friends to leave my house completely content, whether I've just hosted a blow-out bash, a poker party, or a girls' night of chick flicks and gossip. Whatever the occasion, a knockout dessert is sure to bring on happy, sugary smiles!

For a *chica* who doesn't have much of a sweet tooth, though, this is not the easiest trick to pull off. I'm more of a spicy-salty girl than a sweet one, and I prefer cooking to baking. Don't get me wrong, I give in to sugar cravings like anyone else.

My dilemma is this: Though I give in to making, and sometimes eating, desserts, I don't want to have to spend lots of time on them. So when I have to create a dessert, I search out ingredients that will give me the biggest bang for the least fuss. My dessert arsenal is loaded with heavy-duty artillery such as dulce de leche (a *chica's* best friend), frozen puff pastry, canned guava paste, fruit, nuts, sorbet, and ice cream. These are the stars in my cheat-to-win dessert world. With them I can whip up Passion Fruit Mousse (page 241) and twist some pastry Churros (page 237)—indulgent homemade desserts that still give me enough time before the party to take a leisurely stroll with my Yorkie, Salsita. That's my kind of sweet success!

dulce de leche cookie sandwiches (alfajor)

MAKES 16 TO 18 COOKIES

2 cups all-purpose flour, sifted, plus extra for rolling the dough

1/4 cup confectioners' sugar, sifted, plus extra for dusting

1/2 teaspoon salt

1 cup (2 sticks) unsalted butter, cut into small pieces and softened

1 cup dulce de leche, at room temperature

1/4 teaspoon ground cinnamon

1/8 teaspoon ground cloves

Pinch of grated nutmeg

My dad's mother, Tita, made great cookies, and these remind me of hers. For an extra-pretty presentation, neatly stack two or three cookies on top of one another on a dessert plate. Cut a heart or a flower shape out from a piece of paper and place the stencil next to the cookies. Dust confectioners' sugar over your design, remove the paper, and you have a cute added effect. Remember, we eat with our eyes!

1 Preheat your oven to 350°F. Line a baking sheet with parchment paper and set aside.

2 Place the flour, confectioners' sugar, salt, and butter in a medium bowl and work the ingredients together using your fingers or a pastry blender. If the dough is too sticky, add a little more flour so that you can shape the soft dough into a disc. Wrap the dough disc in plastic wrap and refrigerate for 10 to 20 minutes.

3 Sprinkle some flour onto your work surface and roll the dough 1/8 inch thick. Use a 2 1/2-inch round cookie cutter to cut out the cookies. Using a thin spatula, transfer the rounds to your baking sheet. Bring the dough scraps together and gently press into a ball. Flour your work surface, reroll the dough to 1/8 inch thick, and cut out more rounds.

4 Bake the cookies until they are golden and firm, 15 to 20 minutes. Remove the cookies and let them cool for 5 minutes before transferring them to a wire rack to cool completely.

5 Place the dulce de leche in a small bowl and stir in the cinnamon, cloves, and nutmeg. Spread about 1 1/2 teaspoons of the dulce de leche on the flat side of a cookie and sandwich with the flat side of a second cookie. Place the cookies on a platter, dust them with confectioners' sugar, and serve.

three-way brigadeiros truffles

MAKES 18

1 tablespoon unsalted butter, at room temperature

1 14-ounce can sweetened condensed milk

¼ teaspoon coconut extract

1½ tablespoons unsweetened cocoa powder

1½ teaspoons instant espresso powder

¼ cup chocolate sprinkles

¼ cup toasted coconut flakes

¼ cup finely chopped nuts (such as pistachios or almonds)

These are so easy that you'll find yourself making them for any occasion or non-occasion. I like to roll them in three different coatings for a beautiful and impressive presentation. Feel free to use all three, or choose your favorite coating and roll with it!

1 Grease a dinner plate or a baking sheet with half of the softened butter and set aside. Whisk the condensed milk, coconut extract, and cocoa powder together in a small saucepan. Cook over medium heat, stirring constantly, until the milk thickens and a wooden spoon leaves a trail in the bottom of the pan, 15 to 20 minutes. Stir in the espresso powder, pour the mixture out onto the greased plate, and let it cool completely, about 45 minutes.

2 Place the chocolate sprinkles, coconut flakes, and nuts on 3 plates. Grease your hands with the remaining butter and roll a tablespoonful of the chocolate mixture into a ball between your hands. Repeat with the remaining mixture and then roll the balls around in the sprinkles, coconut flakes, and nuts until evenly coated, lightly pressing the coatings in with your fingers to make sure they stick. Arrange the brigadeiros in mini muffin cups or on a platter and serve, or leave them out at room temperature until you're ready to serve them.

pastry twists with dulce de leche and mexican hot chocolate fondue (churros)

SERVES 4 TO 6

1/4 cup sugar

1 tablespoon ground cinnamon

1 sheet of defrosted puff pastry dough

2 2-ounce Ibarra chocolate discs, chopped

1/2 cup cream

1 tablespoon spiced rum

Dulce de leche, warmed

chica tip: This is my short-cut version of churros, which are normally made from scratch and deep fried.

Cinnamon sugar twists are good any time of the day: for breakfast, after dinner, or as a late-night snack. They're not too sweet and are a little starchy, so they're a good combination for someone like me who doesn't have that much of a sweet tooth. They're delicious on their own, and even better with dulce de leche and chocolate sauce for dipping. Serve the sauces in shot glasses so everyone has his or her very own to dip into.

1 Preheat your oven to 375°F. Line a baking sheet with parchment paper and set aside. Mix the sugar with the cinnamon in a small bowl and set aside.

2 Sprinkle some cinnamon sugar on your work surface and place the puff pastry in an even, single layer on top. Brush the pastry lightly with water and sprinkle generously with cinnamon sugar. Flip the pastry over and repeat on the second side. Cut the pastry into 1/2- to 3/4-inch-wide strips. Place them on the prepared baking sheet, twisting the ends of each strip so it looks like a corkscrew. Bake until they're puffed and golden brown, about 20 minutes, and set aside to cool completely.

3 Meanwhile, make the chocolate sauce. Place the chocolate in a small heat-proof bowl and bring the cream to a simmer in a small saucepan. Pour the cream over the chocolate, cover the bowl with plastic wrap, and let sit for 5 minutes. Stir to combine, then add the rum. Serve immediately, or cover to keep warm (or rewarm in the microwave, stirring every 10 seconds, if making ahead).

4 Serve the churros with a bowl of dulce de leche and another bowl of Mexican hot chocolate sauce for dipping.

fruit "salad" (salpicón)

SERVES 8 TO 10

FOR THE CHERRY SYRUP

1 cup sugar

1 cup natural cherry juice

FOR THE SALPICÓN

1 cup papaya balls

1 cup finely chopped pineapple

1 cup watermelon balls

1 cup honeydew or cantaloupe balls

1 cup finely chopped mango (see page 50)

1 cup apple balls

1 cup green or red grapes

1 cup halved orange segments

2 liters chilled club soda

Who can feel guilty about enjoying dessert when it is essentially a healthy fruit salad? Salpicón is the best fruit salad you could imagine, spiked with orange or cherry soda and served in a tall fountain glass. You can use any kind of fruit in this dish; as long as it comes to about 8 cups total, anything goes! If you don't have a melon baller to make the balls of fruit, you can chop it instead. I like to make my own cherry soda for salpicón, but you can substitute 2 liters of natural cherry soda (5½ 12-ounce cans) if you prefer.

1 To make the syrup, bring the sugar and cherry juice to a boil in a small saucepan, stirring often to dissolve the sugar. Transfer to a heat-proof liquid measuring cup, cover with plastic wrap, and refrigerate until cold.

2 To make the salpicón, toss the fruit together in a large bowl. Fill tall glasses with ¾ to 1 cup of fruit and add some cherry syrup. Top off with club soda and serve with a straw and a spoon.

passion fruit mousse (maracuyá)

SERVES 10

2 cups frozen passion fruit pulp, defrosted

4 cups heavy cream

1 14-ounce can sweetened condensed milk

Mint sprigs, for serving

Biscotti or other crisp cookies, for serving

This mousse is from my favorite neighborhood restaurant in Miami, Tutto Pasta. The owner, Juca, is from Brazil and was gracious enough to share the recipe with me. I like serving mousse in fun stemware, such as martini glasses and champagne flutes, or even in old-fashioned diner-style parfait glasses. Even though the mousse takes minutes to make, if you present it with flair, your friends will respond to it in kind. Most any puréed fruit works in this recipe; two of my favorites besides passion fruit are puréed frozen strawberries and raspberries.

1 Place 1 tablespoon of passion fruit pulp in the bottom of 10 martini glasses (you'll use ½ cup total passion fruit pulp) or ramekins and set them aside.

2 Using an electric mixer, beat the cream until it holds stiff peaks. Whisk 1¼ cups of passion fruit pulp with the condensed milk in a large bowl, add one fourth of the whipped cream, and whisk it in. Fold in the remaining whipped cream and fill the martini glasses or ramekins with some of the mousse. Drizzle some of the remaining passion fruit pulp over the top. Serve immediately or cover with plastic wrap and refrigerate for up to 8 hours. Serve cold with a mint sprig and a biscotti.

guava, oaxaca cheese, and
dulce de leche "empanada" cake

SERVES 8

½ tablespoon unsalted butter, at room temperature, or nonstick cooking spray

All-purpose flour, for dusting the work surface

1 17.3-ounce package defrosted puff pastry sheets

¼ cup dulce de leche, at room temperature

4 ounces guava paste, thinly sliced

1 cup grated Oaxaca or mozzarella cheese

1 large egg white, lightly beaten

Sugar (preferably Demerara or turbinado), for sprinkling

Confectioners' sugar, for garnish

chica tip: You can assemble the dessert a few hours in advance, then bake it when everyone sits down for dinner. Serve it while it's still hot and the cheese is all melty and yummy.

This is like a giant dessert empanada made from a puff pastry shell. It's stuffed with caramely dulce de leche, sweet guava paste, and salty-savory Oaxaca cheese. Yum, ¡que rico! While some might consider a dessert made with cheese odd, once you taste the cheese in combination with the guava paste and dulce de leche, you'll get why this sweet-savory combo is a Latin classic!

1 Preheat your oven to 350°F. Line a baking sheet with parchment paper and grease it with the butter or coat with nonstick cooking spray.

2 Sprinkle your work surface with some flour. Place an unfolded sheet of pastry on your work surface and roll it ⅛ inch thick to make a 9 ½- to 10-inch square. Set a 9-inch round cake pan or an upturned dinner plate on top of the pastry and cut around it to make a circle. Transfer the pastry to the prepared baking sheet (save the dough scraps to decorate the top of the pastry, or discard) and repeat with the second sheet of pastry. (After rolling, transfer the second sheet of pastry to a parchment-paper-lined baking sheet or a dinner plate and refrigerate it if your kitchen is very warm.)

3 Spread the first pastry disc with the dulce de leche, leaving a ½- to 1-inch border around the edge. Place the guava slices over the dulce de leche and sprinkle the grated cheese over the guava. Brush the edges of the pastry with the beaten egg white.

4 Set the second pastry disc on top of the grated cheese, press the pastry edges together, then press the tines of an upturned fork around the edge to make a decorative seal. Brush the top of the pastry with the beaten egg white and sprinkle with sugar (decorate with the reserved pastry if you like). Bake until golden brown, about 30 minutes. Let cool for 10 minutes, dust with confectioners' sugar, and serve immediately.

affogato latino

SERVES 4

1 pint vanilla bean ice cream

½ cup dulce de leche liqueur or coffee liqueur

4 shots of brewed espresso

For a real Latin flavor, make this with dulce de leche liqueur. If they don't have it at your local liquor store, then use Irish cream whiskey. Prepare the espresso with an espresso machine or use instant espresso powder—or, better yet, order it from your favorite coffee joint and reheat it just before serving.

1 Chill 4 clear medium heat-proof glasses in the freezer.

2 Scoop ½ cup of ice cream into each chilled glass and top with 2 tablespoons of liqueur. Pour the hot espresso over the ice cream and serve immediately!

cheesecake flan

SERVES 10 TO 12

2 cups sugar

12 ounces cream cheese, at room temperature

3 large eggs, at room temperature

1 14-ounce can sweetened condensed milk

1 12-ounce can evaporated milk

1½ cups whole milk, at room temperature

1 teaspoon vanilla extract

Most people like cheesecake. Most people like flan. Put the two together and you have a dessert most people will love! My best friends from Miami, the Dascal sisters, had a nanny, named Tata, who made them the most fantastic silky-textured cheesecake flan. I begged Tata for the recipe for eighteen years, and she has finally given in! Once you taste it, you'll thank me for being so persistent. Don't be alarmed by the thin consistency of the batter; it's supposed to be a little runny. Clean the leftover hardened caramel in the ramekins by filling each one with boiling water; like magic, the caramel disappears.

1 Place the sugar and ¼ cup of water in a medium saucepan over medium-high heat. Stir the sugar occasionally, being careful not to get any grains stuck against the sides of the saucepan, until it has all dissolved. Swirl the saucepan every minute until the sugar becomes a golden reddish-brown, 10 to 15 minutes. Equally distribute the caramel among 10 to 12 3½-inch ramekins and set aside.

2 Preheat your oven to 325°F.

3 Using an electric mixer, beat the softened cream cheese with the eggs on low speed to combine. Increase the speed to medium high and beat until completely incorporated. Add the condensed milk, evaporated milk, whole milk, and vanilla and continue to beat together until everything is well incorporated, scraping down the sides of the bowl as necessary, 2 to 3 minutes.

(recipe continues)

4 Ladle the custard over the caramel in the ramekins, filling them up to ½ inch from the rim. Place a kitchen towel in a deep baking dish or roasting pan to keep the ramekins from sliding and place the ramekins in two rows on top of the towel. Place the baking dish in the oven and pour enough hot water into the baking dish to reach halfway up the sides of the ramekins, taking care not to get water in the ramekins. Cover the baking dish tightly with aluminum foil and bake until the flan is just set, about 30 minutes (when you tap the edge of a ramekin the flan should still wobble a little in the center).

5 Carefully remove the baking dish from the oven, remove the foil, and let the ramekins cool slightly. Using tongs, remove the ramekins from the water and set on a towel to cool for at least 2 hours before serving. Once it is cooled completely, the flan can be refrigerated for up to 3 days before unmolding and serving. To serve, run a thin knife around the inside edge of the ramekin to loosen the flan, and then invert it onto a plate.

coffee "cortadito" granita

SERVES 4

1¼ cups strong espresso

⅓ cup sweetened condensed milk

3 tablespoons coffee liqueur or whiskey

If you're a fan of Thai coffee, then boy, are you going to love this recipe! It's fantastically simple—much easier than making other frozen desserts. To keep your coffee beans their freshest, store them in your freezer in a tightly sealed bag and grind them in small batches.

1 Whisk the espresso, condensed milk, and coffee liqueur in a small bowl until the sugar is dissolved.

2 Transfer the mixture to an 8-inch square baking dish and freeze until the mixture turns slushy, about 20 minutes (don't let it completely freeze). Remove the granita from the freezer and scrape it up with a fork to make slushy granules, making sure to get into the corners. Place it back into the freezer and repeat scraping it up with a fork every 20 to 30 minutes, or until it is frozen in firm, coarse grains. Serve in small bowls or coffee cups.

eggnog popsicles (coquito)

MAKES 9 POPSICLES

1 13.5-ounce can coconut milk

1 12-ounce can evaporated milk

¾ cup plus 2 tablespoons sweetened condensed milk

⅛ teaspoon salt

1 egg yolk

⅛ teaspoon ground cinnamon

½ teaspoon vanilla extract

¾ cup white rum

Popsicles are the nonbaker's answer to dessert! I love them because they appeal to the kid in me; my friends love them because I spike them with all kinds of fun stuff like rum and tequila. This recipe is based on the Puerto Rican version of eggnog, called coquito. Because I live in a warm climate, I can get away with serving them for dessert even in the wintertime. If you aren't so lucky, serve them as an apéritif for a "Christmas in July" party. Do note that this recipe contains a raw egg yolk, so if you have health concerns regarding raw eggs, you can substitute 2 tablespoons of prepared eggnog.

1 Place all of the ingredients in a blender and blend to combine.

2 Pour the mixture into a popsicle mold, cover, and insert popsicle sticks. Freeze until set.

chica tip: If you don't own a popsicle mold, use 5-ounce disposable paper cups instead. Pour in the mixture and cover the cups with aluminum foil. Insert a popsicle stick in each cup, place the cups in a baking dish, and freeze until set. Discard the foil, peel off the cup, and enjoy.

frozen margarita pops

SERVES 6

½ cup tequila

6 lime all-fruit frozen pops, such as FrozFruit

Margarita salt or kosher salt

Pour the tequila into a tall and narrow glass. Remove the frozen pops from their wrappers and submerge them one by one in the glass of tequila, tilting the glass to completely moisten the entire popsicle. Sprinkle each side of the frozen pops with some salt and then arrange the pops on a plate and serve immediately.

frozen piña colada pops

SERVES 6

½ cup rum (or pineapple juice)

6 coconut all-fruit frozen pops, such as FrozFruit

1 cup Demerara or turbinado sugar

Toasted coconut flakes

To make virgin piña colada popsicles, substitute pineapple juice for the rum.

Pour the rum into a tall and narrow glass. Remove the frozen pops from their wrappers and submerge them one by one in the glass of rum, tilting the glass to completely moisten the entire popsicle. Sprinkle each side of the frozen pops with some sugar, arrange the pops on a plate, sprinkle with the coconut, and serve immediately.

acknowledgments

Thanks to everyone who has trooped alongside me, professionally and personally, throughout all these years. This book wouldn't have happened without all of you.

my family Mom, you are my inspiration. Thanks for sharing and teaching me the joy of life, food, laughter, family, friends, and hard work. Dad, you always encourage me to do what I love, to do my best, and to lead by example. Johanna, thanks for believing in me and helping me get started. Annelies and my brother-in-law Jossy, your support and advice are invaluable. Aunt Marlene Hoffmann, thank you for nurturing my creative side, and to my handsome and sweet nephews Franco, Diego, and Joshua—thank you for making me so proud. Andrew, you stick by me, help me, endure my crazy hours, and love me; for this I can't thank you enough.

To my other moms: the late Celina León, who loved having me in her catering kitchen even when I caused chaos; Tía Magda Martínez, for being my second mom; María Gómez, for letting me pull up a stool to the stove when I was just five years old. My late and dearly missed cousin/best friend/almost brother Sergio Arango—I miss you so.

my friends and chosen family Jackie, Lizzy, Karla, Fanny, Isabel, Christine, Michelle B., Marielena and Melisa Martinez, Marielena Uzcategui, Lisi, Juana, Michelle, Mijanou, Ruby, Ynoluz, Kenneth, Gregory, Cathy; Jackie Watson, for giving me my first food TV gig and for being a friend; and Toni Almeida, for all the motivation training, both mind and body.

my family at chica worldwide Steven Ship, thank you for your vision, creative and business guidance, daily input, and hard, long hours on everything *Delicioso*. Ian Ross, for backing me/us and fueling the plane—thanks for hanging in and putting your money where your mouth is.

Louis and Roz Silverstein, thank you for all of your loving support. My *chicas* at Chica Worldwide: assistant extraordinaire and friend Claudia Uribe Crousillat, you are a first-class trouper; Delia León, you're a real-life wonder woman; Diana Holguín and Alexia Maxwell, thank you.

Thanks to my publicist and trusted friend Rebecca Brooks and all the girls at the Brooks Group: Erica, Amanda, and Brianne, you *chicas* rock; Eric Bergner at Moses and Singer, thanks for taking such good care of me and helping me understand all that mumbo jumbo; to my agent extraordinaire, David Kuhn at Kuhn Projects; and to Lisa Shotland and the gang—Christy, Maggie, and John—at CAA.

my book team A big *gracias* to the entire gang at Clarkson Potter/Random House, especially to Pam Krauss for your great vision, contributions, knowledge, and for believing in me from the get-go; to Jane Treuhaft and Elizabeth Van Itallie for the fabulous design; and to my collaborator Raquel Pelzel, this book would not be without your relentless efforts and passion. Thank you, Andrew Meade, for your brilliant photography (and the patience of a saint!); Stephana Bottom, for being the food police; Barbara Fritz, for the props; David Lutke, Dawn Yanagihara, and J. Scott Wilson, for your help.

my delicioso gang Thanks to Luis Balaguer; Francisco Daza, Conchita Oliva, and the rest of the team at Latin World Entertainment; Julia Dangond, my friend and TV producer, for contributing to making *Simply Delicioso* a reality; Marla Acosta, for making me look good after eighteen hours of grind; the whole team at *BuenHogar,* including my editor, Nahyr Acosta, Julio Hernandez, Ethel Palaci, Sergio Andricain, Linda Rodriguez, Marines Duarte, and Nilda Gomez; Joanne Lynch, Cesar Conde, Margarita Black, and everyone at Galavision; Bob Tuschman, Brooke Johnson, and the whole gang at Food Network; and Kim Yorio at YC Media. At Univision's *Despierta America,* a big thank-you to Mari Garcia Marquez, Victor Santiago, and the whole team for their support.

in good company The following manufacturers and companies have been very generous with their help and support: Calphalon (www.calphalon.com), La Cuisine Gourmet (www.lacuisinegourmet.com), Chelsea Wine Vault, El Latino Foods' Marielena Ibanez, Mac Cosmetics, Etro, Bowery Kitchen, Visiona Kalustyan, Casa Blanca Fish Market, and Milam's Market.

index